Edexcel GCSE
Business:
Introduction to Economic Understanding

Student Book

Keith Hirst • Jonathan Shields
Andrew Ashwin consultant editor

A PEARSON COMPANY

Acknowledgements

Pearson Education Limited
Edinburgh Gate
Harlow
Essex
CM 20 2JE
England
© Pearson Education 2009

The right of Keith Hirst and Jonathan Shields to be identified as the authors of this work has been asserted by them in accordance with the Copyright, Designs and Patents Act 1988.

All rights reserved. No part of this publication may be reproduced, stored in a retrieval system, or transmitted in any form or by any means, electronic, mechanic, photocopying, recording or otherwise without either the prior written permission of the Publishers or a licence permitting restricted copying in the United Kingdom issued by the Copyright Licensing Agency Ltd, 90 Tottenham Court Road, London W1P 9EH

ISBN 978-1-84690-499-8

Graphics by Matthew Waring-Collins
Photography Andrew Allen
Edited by Dave Gray
Proof reading by Mike Kidson

First edition 2009
10 9 8 7 6 5
Page origination by Caroline Waring-Collins, Waring Collins Ltd, Swordfish Business Park, Burscough, Lancs, L40 8JW
Printed in Malaysia, CTP-KHL

We are grateful to the following for permission to reproduce copyright material.
Peter Gately from Nonsolovino in Chesterield for the photograph of the business, Trevor Dakin, owner of Vasco in Wickersley for the photograph of the business, Stuart Collins, photographer for his photographs, Sallyann Kilby of Wharfe Valley Farms for the logo, Lush for the image from the business's website.

The publisher and authors wish to thank the following for photographs used in the production of this book.
Biosphoto/Huguet Pierre p 87, Chris Ratcliffe/Rex Features p 6-7, DigitalVision pp 41 (r), 76, Eye Ubiquitous/Rex Features p 104, Focus/Maximishin/Rex Features p 82 (bl), Fraser Gray/Rex Features p 32, Invicta Kent Media/ Rex Features p 52, Jason Alden/Rex Features p 110, Jonathan Banks/Rex features p 54 (b), Jupiter Unlimited Royalty-Free pp17, 19, 23, 26-27, 36, 46, 48, 54 (t), 55 (b), 57, 59, 60, 63 (l), 65, 67, 71, 80, 82 (tl), 82 (br), 88, 91, 92, 98-99, 100, 101, 103, 106, KPA/Zuma/Rex Features p 35, LEHTIKUVA OY/Rex Features p 84, Marco Secchi/Rex Features p 111, Martin Lee/Rex features p 62, Nick Cunard/ Rex Features p53, Phil Rees/Rex Features p 63 (r), Philippe Hayes/Rex Features p 69, Photodisc pp 21 (t), 82 (tr), 85, Richard Gardner/Rex Features p 55 (t), Richard Sowesby/Rex Features p 66, Shutterstock pp 8, 9, 10, 12, 15, 18, 20, 21 (b), 79, 114, 119, Solent News/Rex Features p 61, Stockbyte p 22, 41 (l), Thomas Hegenbart/Rex Features p 108.

Thanks
Thanks to the people and businesses who have contributed so willingly to the book. Peter Gately from Nonsolovino in Chesterield, Trevor Dakin, owner of Vasco in Wickersley and Stuart Collins, photographer. Sallyann Kilby of Wharfe Valley Farms has been extremely generous with her time and support. Thanks also to colleagues within the Humanities faculty, especially Andrew Refern and Neil Plant, for their continued good advice and support. Business and Economics students from Wickersley School and Sports College have provided much of the inspiration for the content. Finally, thanks to Audrey, George, Laura and Millie – who have complained only infrequently about the time the project has taken and the family time it has cost. Keith Hirst

I would like to thank Andrew Ashwin for providing his constructive critique of both the text and questions. David Gray at Pearson was also legendary in both his professionalism and willingness to be highly flexible with deadlines, without whom I would have descended into a mire of work. I would also like to thank my co-author Keith Hirst for his input which made this textbook a true collaborative effort. Most of all I would like to thank my wife Tamsyn, my daughter Tamar and my son Rowan. Without their patience, support, love and understanding I would never have had the mental capacity to complete this project. Jonathan Shields

I would like to thank all my colleagues at Biz/ed for supporting me in doing this project, specifically Andy Hargrave, Jill Jones, Stewart Perrygrove and John Yates. There are many people who worked on the development of the qualification on which this book is based. Their faith, support, encouragement and considerable hard work and skill were crucial in getting the qualification live. As a result thanks go to Susan Hoxley, Kelly Padwick, Beverley Anim-Antwi, Derek Richardson and Lizzie Firth. No book would be produced without the dedication of the authors who combine considerable work pressures with the task of producing the book and supporting materials, mostly in their own time. The fact that the production process has been relatively trouble free is largely due to their dedication, commitment, professionalism and support. Thanks go to Alain Anderton, Ian Gunn, Keith Hirst, Andrew Malcolm, Jonathan Shields and Nicola Walker for their contributions and effort. At Pearson, Dave Gray has been a much valued publisher - his skill in handling people, deadlines, vast quantities of text and queries, whilst retaining patience and humour, has been invaluable. It has been a privilege to work with you Dave - thank you. Finally, thanks go to my family, Sue, Alex and Johnny for their patience and love. Andrew Ashwin 2009

Contents: delivering the EDEXCEL GCSE Business (Introduction to Economic Understanding) Specification Unit 5

Introduction	**4**
Topic 5.1 How can I start to think like an economist?	**6**
1 What trade-offs exist?	8
2 Does raising or lowering price always work?	12
3 Do all stakeholders have the same perspective?	16
4 Are there any hidden costs or benefits?	20
Exam zone featuring results plus	24
Topic 5.2 Risk or certainty?	**26**
5 How can success be measured?	28
6 What causes business failure?	32
7 What problems does the economy face?	36
8 How important are exchange rates?	42
9 Can the government solve economic and social problems?	46
Exam zone featuring results plus	50
Topic 5.3 Big or small?	**52**
10 How do businesses grow?	54
11 Why do businesses grow?	58
12 Monopoly power – good or bad?	62
13 Can big business be controlled?	66
Exam zone featuring results plus	72
Topic 5.4 Is growth good?	**74**
14 What is growth?	76
15 Does growth increase the standard of living?	80
16 Can growth be bad?	84
17 Can growth be sustainable?	88
18 What can the government do?	92
Exam zone featuring results plus	96
Topic 5.5 Is the world fair?	**98**
19 Is everybody equal?	100
20 Can international trade help?	104
21 Is there any other help?	108
Exam zone featuring results plus	112
Exam zone	**114**
Zone in: Getting into the perfect mental zone for revision	114
Planning zone: How to plan your revision effectively	115
Know zone: All the facts you need to know and exam-style practice	116
Don't panic zone: Last-minute revision tips	119
Exam zone: Understanding the questions and meet the exam paper	120
Zone out: What happens after the exam	122
Index	**124**

Welcome to the Edexcel GCSE Business Studies series

This series has been written to fully support Edexcel's new GCSE Business Studies qualification, from September 2009. The authors are an experienced team who include senior examiners involved in developing the Edexcel specification, and who have experience of teaching the subject in a range of different schools. The books include lots of engaging features to enthuse students and provide the range of support needed to make teaching and learning a success for all ability levels. The student books in the series are:

- **Introduction to Small Business** covering Units 1 and 2 (compulsory for the Full Course) and Unit 6 (for the Short Course)
- **Building a business** (Unit 3)
- **Business Communications** (Unit 4)
- **Introduction to Economic Understanding** (Unit 5)

Introduction to Economic Understanding

Unit 5: The specification presents an opportunity to study some introductory economics as part of a Business Studies qualification. This book mirrors the concept-based approach found in the specification, and uses stimulating and engaging topics to help see relevant everyday situations from an economist's point of view. From here students will be able to transfer their thinking skills to other topics they come across. This book introduces some of the key economic concepts and thinking that will help to build confidence for tackling the subject in post-16 education and the world of work.

How to use this book

Each Edexcel GCSE Business Studies unit is divided into topics. These books are written in the same easy-to-follow format, with each topic split into digestible chapters. You will find these features in each chapter:

Topic overview A case study sets the scene for each topic, accompanied by a series of questions. Your teacher might look at this as a starter activity to find out what you already know about the subject. You'll find a summary of the assessment for the topic.

Content and objectives Each chapter starts with a case study to put the content in a context, followed by the objectives for that chapter.

Edexcel key terms are highlighted and defined in each chapter.

Test yourself question practice in every chapter contains objective and multiple choice questions.

Over to you question practice in every chapter. A short case study is followed by questions written in exam paper style.

A dedicated suite of revision resources for complete exam success We've broken down the six stages of revision to ensure you are prepared every step of the way.

Zone in: How to get into the perfect 'zone' for revision.

Planning zone: Tips and advice on how to effectively plan revision.

Know zone: The facts you need to know, memory tips and exam-style practice at the end of every topic.

Don't panic zone: Last-minute revision tips.

Exam zone: What to expect on the exam paper and the key terms used.

Zone out: What happens after the exams.

ResultsPlus

These features are based on knowledge of how students have performed in past exams. They draw on expert advice and guidance from examiners to show you how to achieve better results.

There are four different types of ResultsPlus features throughout this book:

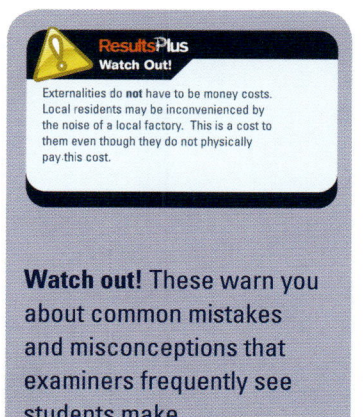

Watch out! These warn you about common mistakes and misconceptions that examiners frequently see students make.

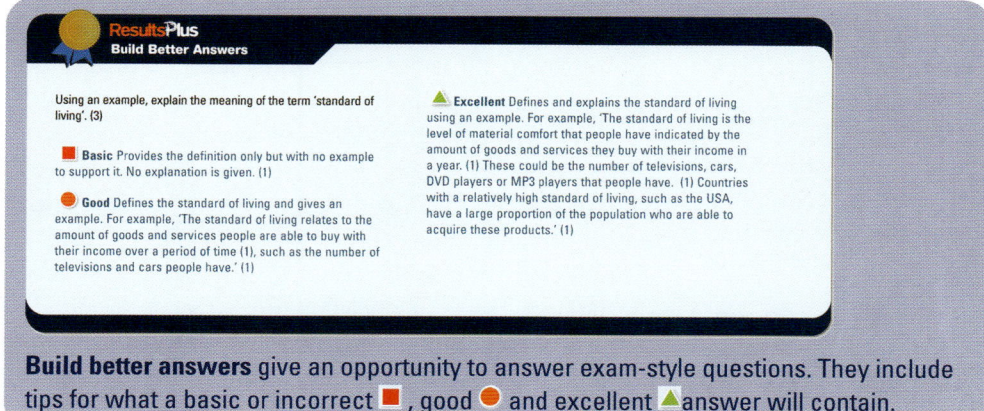

Build better answers give an opportunity to answer exam-style questions. They include tips for what a basic or incorrect ■, good ● and excellent ▲ answer will contain.

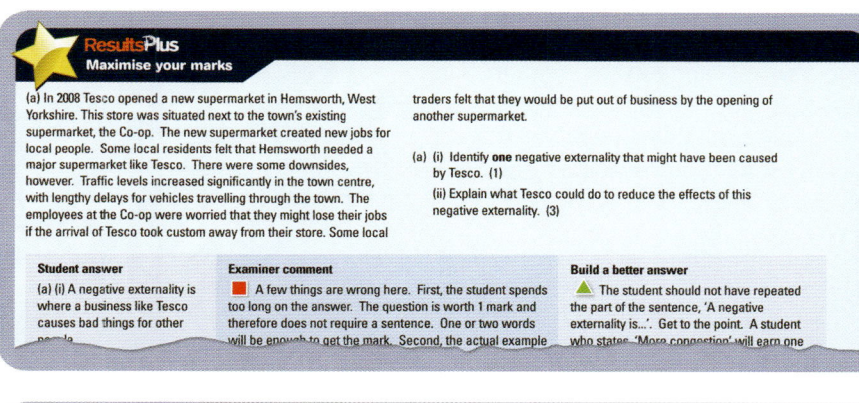

Maximise your marks are featured in the Know Zone at the end of each topic. They include an exam-style question with a student answer, examiner comments and an improved answer so that you can see how to build a better response.

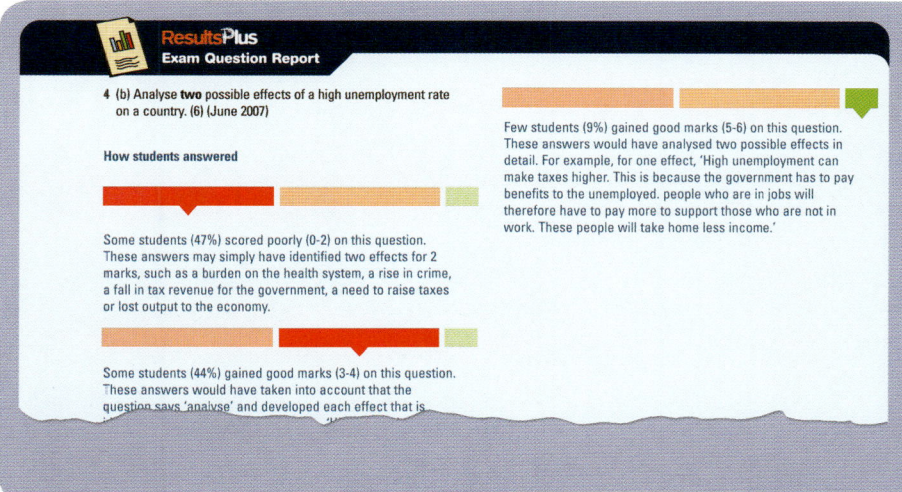

Exam question reports show previous exam questions with details about how well students answered them.
- Red shows the number of students who scored low marks
- Orange shows the number of students who did okay
- Green shows the number of students who did well.

They explain how students could have achieved the top marks so that you can make sure that you answer these questions correctly in future.

Assessment

Information on external examinations is covered in the Examzone at the end of the book. This provides details on assessment for the Unit 5 (see pages 120-121).

Topic 5.1: How can I start to think like an economist?

Case study

In 2005 London beat off fierce competition from Paris to win the right to host the 2012 Summer Olympic and Paralympic Games. Winning the race to host the games kick started a billion pound project to build the stadiums, transport infrastructure and buildings necessary to host one of the biggest events on Earth. It was hoped that the new Olympic Park would transform the borough of Newham in London from one of the poorest parts of the city into one of the richest. It was expected that the new road and rail links and the re-generation of the area following the Olympics would attract new businesses, leading to the creation of jobs, boosting the area's wealth and prosperity. However, not everyone was happy with the re-development of Newham. Many businesses and householders were forcibly re-located by the need to allow the Olympic venues to be built. Some businesses were unable to find new buildings in the local area and had to close. Some homeowners that were forcibly moved away were unable to find houses at an affordable price.

However the impacts of the Olympics go much wider than this and many stakeholder groups could be affected throughout the United Kingdom. The cost of staging the Olympics had increased by 2009 and there was a real worry that the final bill could be as high as £10 billion. As hosting the Games became more expensive, there was also concern over whether government spending would be diverted away from other projects. For instance, 23% of the funding for the Olympics comes from the National Lottery. This means that the Arts, Community Groups and other worthy causes could see their funding reduced. There were also worries over whether it is fair for so much money to be spent in London when residents in other parts of the United Kingdom would see limited benefits. With a brand new hospital costing in the region of £400 million, the trade-off created by the Olympics for the whole country could be large, since £10 billion of spending could provide 25 brand new state of the art hospitals across the UK. Supporters of the Olympics argued that the games would, like the Sydney Olympics in 2000, make a profit, since 7.7 million tickets were expected to be sold. However as costs soared, it was expected that the price of the tickets would rise well above what most people could afford and the Olympics would become an experience which only the rich could enjoy.

Source: adapted from www.taxpayersalliance.co.uk, www.politics.co.uk/news/domestic-policy

Topic overview

This topic introduces many key themes in economics about how to make a choice between alternatives and the costs and benefits of making that choice on different groups of people. 'Should government spend more on hospitals? If it does, what are the costs or trade-offs involved? How does a firm decide whether or not to buy more machinery or spend more money on training its workers? These are all important decisions that are made every day across the country. By thinking like an economist, the chances of making the right decision are increased since you have considered the size of any benefits or costs that arise from the decision made. You also examine the extent to which these benefits and costs impact on others.

1. In what ways could the residents of Newham benefit from the building of the Olympic Park in their borough?
2. (a) Which groups of people could be disadvantaged by the decision to allow London to host the Olympic Games?
   (b) In what ways could these groups of people be disadvantaged?
3. Should the organisers increase the price of tickets to cover the increased costs of staging the Olympic Games? Justify your answer.

5.1 How can I start to think like an economist?

What will I learn?

What trade-offs exist? Why are we forced to make choices and decisions? What are the consequences of making a decision? What are the trade-offs and opportunity costs involved when we choose one thing over another?

Does raising or lowering the price always work? Why do some firms increase their prices, when other firms have to decrease theirs? What happens to revenue when a firm changes its prices? What makes demand price sensitive or price insensitive?

Do all stakeholders have the same perspective? What are stakeholders? Why is there often a conflict of interest between different groups of people on the same issue? What decides who wins and how is the conflict resolved?

Are there any hidden costs or benefits? What are negative and positive externalities? What are the costs and benefits of a firm's activities that it does not consider?

How will I be assessed?

Unit 5 is assessed by a 1 hour 30 minute written examination consisting of three sections. Section A contains multiple choice and short answer questions designed to test your knowledge and understanding of the specification. Sections B and C use pieces of evidence and will include short answer questions together with some extended writing questions. The extended writing questions are designed to focus on the higher order skills of analysis and evaluation.

1 What trade-offs exist?

Case Study

Daniel Michaels was reaching the end of Year 9. He knew that he had to pick his GCSE subjects soon. His school was providing him with a choice of Geography, History, ICT, Photography and Art. From this list Daniel had to pick two subjects. He decided that the best way to choose was to write a list of his own, with his favourite option subject at the top and least favourite option subject at the bottom. This, he felt, would make it easier to make the right choice.

Objectives

- To understand that the basic economic problem is one of trying to meet unlimited needs with limited resources.
- To understand that economics is about making choices.
- To appreciate that making choices involves having to make sacrifices.
- To understand the trade-offs that have to be made when making choices.
- To recognise that the meaning of cost is more than giving up money.
- To understand that when making choices we place values on these choices.
- To apply the key concepts of trade-offs and opportunity costs to a variety of contexts.

Making a choice

After speaking to teachers and students in Year 10, Daniel felt he had enough information to create his list, which is shown in Table 1. He decided to choose Geography, which he had always really enjoyed. His second choice was more difficult because he was interested in both History and ICT. Ideally he would have liked to study three subjects. The school told Daniel that this was not possible, since they did not have enough teachers and classrooms to allow Year 10 to make three choices. In the end Daniel chose ICT for his second subject. Without realising it Daniel had just discovered the basic economic problem.

- Daniel wanted to choose more subjects than he was able to - this relates to human needs.
- The school did not have enough teachers, classrooms or time to provide all these subjects. This shows that we have limited resources.
- Because the resources were not enough to satisfy all Daniels needs he had to make a **choice**.

By writing a list of subjects to help him place a value on his options, Daniel had shown that he was already starting to think like an economist.

The basic economic problem is that of **scarcity** of resources. In this case Daniel's school did not have enough teachers and classrooms to allow him to study History as well. Therefore Daniel was forced into making a choice. By choosing ICT instead of History, Daniel also faced a **trade-off**. He had to give up the benefits of one option (studying history) to gain the benefits from another - studying ICT. Economists would assume that Daniel must have placed a greater value on studying ICT rather than History. He was sacrificing his knowledge of History to be able to become good with computers by studying ICT.

People face the basic economic problem of scarcity and choice every day. It could be something as simple as deciding what to do after the school day has finished. Sarah is Daniel's friend. Her options might be going to the cinema with friends or staying in and completing some homework. In this case, the scarce resource is time since there may not be the time available to do both. If Sarah chooses to go to the cinema, she may believe the benefits of watching the film and being with friends are greater than the benefits of doing her homework.

edexcel key terms

Choice – a decision between one or more alternatives.

Scarcity – resources are limited in supply, e.g. raw materials, time.

Trade-off – where the selection of one choice results in the loss of another.

Sarah's parents, on the other hand, will probably encourage her to do her homework since they believe that the benefit of doing homework is going to be greater than the benefit gained from a night at the cinema. Sarahs view of the trade-off is different to that of her parents.

Cost is more than giving up money

The economic problem is all about making choices. A choice means there are at least two options. When deciding between two options we sub-consciously place values on each before making a decision. Another of Daniel's friends, Ziggy, is faced with the choice of two computer games. He would like them both but can only afford one. His choice is between 'Need for Speed: Undercover' and 'Football Director'. Both are priced at £24.99.

Ziggy chooses to buy 'Need for Speed: Undercover'. In normal speech we would say that the game had 'cost Ziggy £24.99'. However, in economics, money is only a means of exchange - the way in which goods and services are acquired. The real cost to Ziggy was that, in making his choice, he had to sacrifice 'Football Director'. Ziggy had to trade-off the benefits of 'Football Director' for the benefits he would gain from 'Need for Speed: Undercover'. Again, economists would assume that Ziggy valued the benefits from the game he chose above those of the game he sacrificed. The true cost of making a choice is not the money given up but the alternative that has been sacrificed.

Making decisions and suffering trade-offs causes people to experience what is called **opportunity cost**. This measures the value of the benefits you have lost through making a particular decision. For instance, by choosing to study ICT in Year 10, Daniel experienced an opportunity cost, since he could no longer study his third favourite choice History. Equally, in deciding to go to the cinema, Sarahs opportunity cost is the inability to spend the time doing homework.

Therefore, opportunity cost measures the size of the trade-off experienced when making a particular decision, measured in terms of the loss of the next most desired alternative.

What decisions do businesses make?

Businesses make lots of decisions every day. With every decision comes a trade-off and an opportunity cost. They may have to decide between opening new stores or spending on marketing, for example. In 2007, Topshop paid the supermodel, Kate Moss, £3 million pounds to design a range of clothes that they would sell in each of their 225 stores. In deciding to pay Kate Moss £3 million, Topshop would have considered whether or not the trade-off and opportunity costs of doing this were too large. For instance, the £3 million pounds could have been used by Topshop to open new stores or refurbish their existing ones. Topshop must have believed that the value of the benefits that they would gain from signing up Kate Moss would be greater than the value of the benefits gained from using the £3 million any other way. In the end the opportunity cost of paying Kate Moss £3 million was small, since her clothing range ended up being highly profitable for Topshop.

What decisions do Governments make?

Just like individuals and businesses, the Government also has to make difficult choices due to the scarcity of resources. For instance, the Government only has a limited amount of money which it raises through taxation and borrowing. It needs to decide how to spend this money, but by making a decision it also faces a trade-off and opportunity cost. You will notice that there are always individuals, groups and businesses telling the Government they should be spending more on one thing or another. The Government, like everyone else, has limited resources but faces almost unlimited demands. It has to make choices.

Businesses may need to make a choice between opening new stores and spending on marketing

ResultsPlus Watch Out!

Do not express opportunity costs in terms of money. Instead express it as the loss of the next best alternative good or service. For instance, the opportunity cost of a holiday priced at £1,500 might be the loss of a new sofa, not the loss of £1,500.

edexcel key terms

Opportunity cost – the loss of the next most desired alternative when choosing a particular course of action.

1 What trade-offs exist?

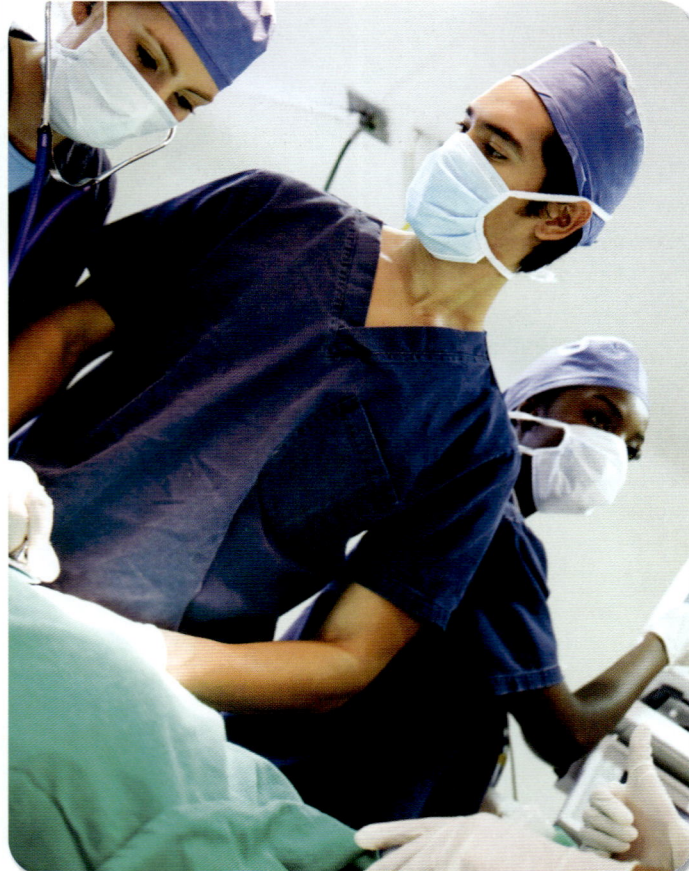

Government may need to make a choice between spending on defence and health

In 2008 the UK Government made the decision to build two new aircraft carriers for the Royal Navy. It is expected that these two new ships will enter service in 2016. Both ships will have a crew of 1,450 sailors and will measure almost 300 meters long. The estimated price of these two ships the government will have to pay is £3.2 billion. In making this decision the Government faced large trade-offs and opportunity costs. For instance the £3.2 billion could have been spent on education and would have allowed them to build 86 new secondary schools in the UK. As a result, the opportunity cost of two new aircraft carriers is the loss of 86 new schools. Again, economists would assume that the government valued the benefits from buying the two ships as being greater than the value of the benefits from the 86 schools.

One of the difficulties (and exciting things) about economics is that everyone has a different view about value. There will be plenty of people who would argue that the Government should have spent their money on schools rather than ships.

Table 1 – Daniel's list

1. Geography
2. ICT
3. History
4. Art
5. Photography

Test yourself

1. Look at Daniel's list in Table 1. If the school had allowed Daniel to make three choices, which **one** of the following would be the opportunity cost Daniel faced by selecting History? Select **one** answer.

    A Photography
    B ICT
    C Art
    D Geography

2. The basic economic problem is that of:

    A having enough money
    B understanding the banking system
    C scarcity of resources and the need to make choices
    D having to work out the financial value of making a choice

    Select **one** answer.

3. In July 2006 Arsenal Football Club moved from Highbury to the new Emirates Stadium 500 metres away in North London. The move cost the club £430 million and not everyone was happy with the amount spent. One Arsenal fan highlighted this by pointing out that the £430 million would have purchased 14 Wayne Rooneys if they had decided not to move. A spokesperson for Arsenal confirmed that the move to the new stadium was an important long-term goal to improve the success of the football club. It is expected that the new stadium will increase Arsenal's profitability since the new stadium has almost 22,000 more seats.

    Source: adapted from www.arsenal.com.

    Which **one** of the following best describes the opportunity cost faced by Arsenal football club in deciding to move to the new stadium? Select **one** answer.

    A The spending of £430 million
    B The benefit of 22,000 more seats
    C The loss of the old Highbury stadium
    D The inability to purchase new players

Over to you

Plymouth City Council is considering spending £44 million pounds building a brand new 'Life Centre'. Inspired by the success of young Plymouth diver, Tom Daley, the centre will include a 50 metre swimming pool, diving pool, ice rink and bowling green. A spokesperson for Plymouth City Council said that the aim is to create a centre for excellence in swimming and diving. However, many groups of people in Plymouth are against the scheme. They feel that £44 million is too much and that the money would be better spent on other council services such as old people's homes and transport.

Source: adapted from http://www.plymouth.gov.uk/homepage/leisureandtourism/sportand recreation/lifecentre.htm.

1. Which of the following would be an opportunity cost faced by Plymouth City Council if it built the Life Centre? Select **one** answer. (1)
A The loss of £44 million
B The loss of spending on other council services
C The cost of buying equipment for the Life Centre
D The cost of employing the staff for the Life Centre
2. Identify **two** problems that might result from Plymouth City Council spending £44 million pounds on the new Life Centre. (2)
3. Many groups of people are against the building of the Life Centre. Explain why large numbers of pensioners are against the scheme. (3)

ResultsPlus
Exam Question Report

On Wednesday 6th July 2005, there were celebrations throughout the country as it was announced that the 2012 Olympic Games would be held in London. The estimated cost of putting on the Games was £2,400 million. Much of this money would be spent on building new facilities in Stratford, East London. The work involved in developing the sites for the Games would be carried out by organisations in both the private sector and the public sector.

- A new hospital in Manchester - a so-called super hospital - was estimated to have cost £400 million in 2001.
- The cost of building a new primary school in Worcestershire was estimated at £1.5 million, the capital cost of a new secondary school in Wales, £13 million.
- The average cost of constructing one mile of a three-lane motorway in 1998 was estimated at £17 million.

Source: http://www.bized.co.uk/current/mind/2004_5/221104.htm

1 (g) Using **one** piece of the information above, estimate the opportunity cost of staging the London Olympics. Show your workings. (4) (June 2007)

How students answered

Most students (88%) scored poorly (0-1) on this question. These answers did not follow the instructions to use the information to estimate the opportunity cost of staging the Olympics. Some answers incorrectly subtracted the cost of a new school or hospital from the cost of the Olympics.

Few students (3%) gained good marks (2-3) on this question. These answers used the instructions. They defined opportunity cost. Many chose the super-hospital example and explained that, for the opportunity cost of the Olympics, 600 hospitals could have been built. But they did not show workings.

Few students (9%) gained very good marks (4) on this question. These answers used a calculation to illustrate the opportunity cost of the Olympics. Most chose the super-hospital example (£400 million). They showed that for the cost of the Olympics (£2,400 million), 600 super-hospitals could have been built (£2,400m ÷ £400m).

2 Does raising or lowering the price always work?

Case Study

Every June, Worthy Farm in Somerset gets invaded by thousands of music fans for the annual Glastonbury Music Festival. Since it began in 1970 the festival has grown steadily and the demand for tickets has increased. When the festival began in 1970 it attracted 1,500 visitors each paying a price of £1. By 2009 the ticket price had increased to £175 and 177,000 people were expected to come and watch the 400 live music acts booked over the five days of the festival. The Glastonbury Festival is now seen by many young people as a must do event with large numbers of students visiting after they have finished their exams in June. In recent years the festivals tickets have sold out in advance with profits from the event being donated to local charities.

Objectives

- To have a clear understanding of the meaning of the term 'price'.
- To define the term revenue and know how to calculate it.
- To understand that the amount of revenue earned depends on how demand reacts to changes in price.
- To understand the difference between 'price sensitivity' and 'price insensitivity'.
- To understand the factors that can influence how price sensitive a product is.

edexcel key terms

Price – the amount of money required to purchase a good or service.

Revenue – the value of sales in a time period, calculated by Price x Quantity Sold.

Demand – the quantity of a good or service a consumer would like to buy at a given price in a time period.

Increasing or decreasing the price?

Michael Eavis, the owner of Worthy Farm and organiser of the Glastonbury Festival, has always had difficulty deciding what price to charge for tickets. The **price** is the amount that has to be handed over by the buyer in exchange for the good or service. In this case, the money handed over is exchanged for a ticket that permits the holder to see a wide range of music acts and other attractions at the festival. It has been suggested that the farm has already reached its capacity. If this is the case then it is difficult to see the festival growing beyond the 177,000 visitors who already attend, due to worries about the safety of festival goers. In deciding the price, Michael has to decide on the amount of **revenue** he needs to raise to cover the cost of staging the event and to make a profit for the local charities.

Michael can calculate the revenue by multiplying the price of the tickets by the number of tickets for sale. If he charged a price of £175 for a ticket and sold all 177,000, he would generate £30,975,000 in revenue. In recent years, some younger festival goers have complained that ticket prices are too high and that the festival is being hi-jacked by older middle class people who can afford to pay higher prices. Michael may want to consider what might happen if he raised or lowered ticket prices.

Lowering the price

If Michael were to lower the price of the tickets, **demand** would increase, but his farm might only be able to cope with 177,000 festival goers and he can already sell all 177,000 tickets at a price of £175. Therefore, if he reduced the price of the tickets to £150 the revenue made by the festival would fall to £26,550,000 since the farm may not be able to cope with more than 177,000 people. Michael needs to consider his price carefully because the cost of staging the festival rises each year. The cost of security, catering, staging, lighting, not to mention the acts themselves, is very high. In 2007, the cost of staging the event was £21,200,000.

Increasing the price

By raising the price of the tickets Michael would be able to increase the revenue and profits made from the festival. This is because if he were to increase the price of the tickets to £200, he knows that demand would probably fall. However, the popularity of the festival is such that he may expect demand to fall by only a small amount - if at all. If he increased price to £200 per ticket demand might fall to 175,000, for example. Festival goers would rather spend less on other things than not go to the festival. This is a good example of **price insensitivity**. This means that demand or sales do not change very much in response to a change in price. In this case the increase in price of £25 might only cause a small fall in the demand for tickets, which could lead to increased revenues. The revenue would be 175,000 x £200 = £35,000,000. The effect of changing the price on the revenues at the Glastonbury Festival is summarised in Table 1.

Table 1 – Changes in price of Glastonbury tickets and possible changes in revenue

Original price of £175 x 177,000 tickets = £30,975,000
Lowering the price to £150 with the attendance remaining the same = £150 x 177,000 tickets = £26,550,000
Increasing the price to £200 with attendance falling only slightly, for example to 175,000 = £200 x 175,000 tickets = £35,000,000.

Revenue is **not** the same as profit. Changing the price may increase or decrease revenues - it all depends how price sensitive demand is.

What makes demand become price insensitive?

Remember that price is the amount of money that is given up in exchange for a good or service. When money is given up consumers are paying to receive the benefits of the good or service. These benefits have a value to the buyer. When a good is purchased the amount the buyer is prepared to hand over in payment (the price) tells us something about the value that the buyer places on consuming the good or service.

In the case of the Glastonbury Music Festival, consumers may feel that £200 represents good value for money - many will feel that the benefit they get from the five days of the festival is easily worth handing over £200 to acquire. In this case demand is price insensitive because festival goers viewed the tickets as a **necessity**. This meant that from their point of view there were few **substitutes** available to them. This is because buying something else with their money would not give them the same enjoyment as going to the Glastonbury Festival. It is the lack of available substitutes which can make demand price insensitive. This then provides the business with the opportunity to increase prices which then leads to a rise in revenue.

It is important for businesses to have some idea of the degree to which the demand for their product or service is sensitive to changes in price. Many businesses use price as a means of influencing revenue and therefore profit. If they have some idea of the price sensitivity of demand for their product it helps them in making decisions that are likely to lead to successful results. Many firms will try different ways to try to make their product more price insensitive - to make consumers believe that the product is important or necessary. Advertising and branding may be ways in which businesses do this; they will want consumers to choose their product over those of rivals - and keep on choosing. This is why customer loyalty is so important.

Price and cost are **not** the same. Price relates to the amount we pay to purchase a product. Cost on the other hand is the amount the firm has to spend to manufacture the product.

edexcel key terms

Price insensitivity – where changing the price of a product by a certain amount leads to a smaller change in demand.

Necessity – a good or service that a consumer views as essential.

Substitute – a good or service which is a possible alternative to another good or service.

2 Does raising or lowering the price always work?

What about price sensitivity?

Price sensitivity is the opposite of price insensitivity. This is where changing the price by a certain amount causes a big reaction by buyers and a larger change in demand. For instance, if Michael had increased the price to £200 per ticket and demand fell to 50,000, for example, ticket revenue would fall to £10,000,000. For this to happen people would perhaps view the festival as 'nothing special' and 'not that good'. Instead people would rather spend money on substitutes like a holiday or going to the Reading Festival instead of buying a more expensive ticket to Glastonbury.

This case study shows that changing the price is not an easy decision to make. In times of falling sales one of the first reactions of many businesses might be to reduce price. This may lead to a rise in revenue but, as highlighted above, not always. Businesses seek to find out how price sensitive demand is for their product before deciding whether to increase or decrease price. In order to do this they often have to undertake market research.

Source: adapted from www.glastonburyfestivals.co.uk.

Price sensitivity – where changing the price by a certain amount results in a bigger change in demand.

Test yourself

1. The demand for Glastonbury Festival Tickets is price insensitive. This means that when the price is increased:

   A   profit increases
   B   revenue decreases
   C   profit decreases
   D   revenue increases

   Select **one** answer.

2. Which **one** of the following would be most likely to make the demand for a good or service price sensitive? Select **one** answer.

   A   If the number of substitutes was limited
   B   High levels of profit
   C   The availability of large numbers of substitutes
   D   If the demand for the product was very strong

3. A firm has discovered through its market research that demand for the product it sells is price sensitive. In order to increase revenues the firm should:

   A   decrease costs
   B   increase prices
   C   increase costs
   D   decrease prices

   Select **one** answer.

ResultsPlus — Build Better Answers

In November 2007 Sony cut the price of its Playstation 3 (PS3) by 16 per cent in the USA. Many thought it was too highly priced. Sony suggested that sales more than doubled as a result of the price cut. Price sensitivity affected how much demand fell.

Source: adapted from www.gameguru.in, www.emagi.co.uk

(a) Identify **one** factor that could affect price sensitivity. (1)
(b) Explain how this factor could have affected the demand for Playstation 3. (3)

Think: What is price sensitivity? What affects price sensitivity? How does this affect how demand reacts to a change in price?

🟥 **Basic** Mentions one factor but offers no explanation or an incorrect explanation. (1)

🟠 **Good** Identifies one factor and offers some explanation that shows how it might affect the demand for PS3. The explanation offers up to 2 basic links to show the effect. A basic link would be there is a number of substitute products for PS3 which could make it price sensitive. (2 - 3)

🔺 **Excellent** Identifies one factor and offers an explanation that shows how it might affect the demand for PS3. The explanation offers up to 3 basic links to show the effect. For example, there is a number of substitute products for PS3, which could make it price sensitive, so demand for PS3 has risen proportionately more than the fall in price. (4)

2 Does raising or lowering the price always work?

Over to you

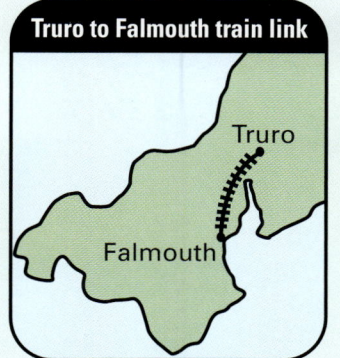

Heather Miller lives in Croydon, South London. Every weekday Heather travels into Central London by Southern trains for the 10 mile journey to work. She has to arrive at work by 8.30 am, and her train journey takes 17 minutes. Her weekly season ticket is priced at £30.50. Every so often, Heather drives to work, but the journey can take as long as an hour and car parking for the whole day can be as much as £10. Trams and buses are also an alternative, but they are also very slow.

400 miles away in Cornwall, Mohammed Humsi makes a different 10 mile trip to work by train during the rush hour. Mohammed is travelling from Falmouth to Truro using Great Western trains. His weekly train ticket is priced at £12.30, almost 60% less for the same distance of journey as Heather. Mohammed also has the option of using alternative modes of transport, he can use the frequent bus services and the roads are seldom busy, giving him the ability to drive to work. Heather suspects her train company is exploiting the price insensitivity of demand on her route.

1. Which of the following best describes demand which is price **in**sensitive? Select **one** answer. (1)
   A When price increases demand increases by a smaller amount
   B When price decreases, demand increases by a larger amount
   C When price increases, demand decreases by a smaller amount
   D When price decreases, demand decreases by a larger amount
2. State **two** possible reasons for the Croydon to London fare being more expensive than the Truro to Falmouth fare, despite the journey being the same distance. (2)
3. Explain the possible effect on Southern trains profits if it exploits price insensitivity of demand. (3)

3 Do all stakeholders have the same perspective?

Case Study

In October 2008 Long Clawson Dairy Limited took over Dairy Crests Stilton cheese making business, Millway. Both companies produce high quality Stilton cheese. As part of the takeover, Long Clawson will close down Hartington Creamery in Derbyshire, one part of the Millway business. This will lead to the loss of 180 jobs at the Hartington plant, as work is moved to Long Clawson's more efficient premises in Leicestershire. The Government is concerned about the take-over as this will lead to a monopoly in the production of Stilton cheese. Long Clawson Dairy Ltd now be only one of two producers making Stilton cheese, the other being Tuxford and Tebbutt. The Competition Commission has launched an investigation to consider whether the takeover was in the public interest.

Objectives

- To define what is mean by a stakeholder and give examples.
- To know what is meant by 'conflict of interest'.
- To be able to give examples of conflicts of interest.
- To be able to explain different stakeholder perspectives of a specific issue or event.
- To be able to analyse and evaluate issues/events from different perspectives.

edexcel key terms

Stakeholders – groups which are interested in the performance of a business.

Shareholders – the owners of a limited company. They buy shares which represent part ownership of a company.

Competition Commission – the body which investigates cases where firms merge or are taken over to decide whether such activity is in the public interest. It has the power to prevent mergers or take-overs where these are seen to reduce the level of competition.

Dividends – the payments made to shareholders from the profits of a company.

Who are stakeholders?

Stakeholders are groups which are interested in the performance of a business. In this example different stakeholder groups can be clearly identified.

- The **shareholders** of Long Clawson were pleased with the takeover as it meant a greater share of the market for Stilton cheese.
- **Workers** at their Leicestershire site were also pleased because it made their jobs more secure.
- **Customers**, on the other hand, now face the prospect of fewer products to choose from. With one dominant business they were worried that the price of their favourite cheese may rise.
- The **Government** has an interest in the case, as the **Competition Commission** has launched an investigation into this takeover.
- The **workers** at Hartington Creamery were directly affected, as the business was to be closed down and all jobs lost.
- This would also have an impact on the **local community**. As a small village, the loss of such an important and major employer would have knock-on effects for other local businesses.

Different stakeholders - different interests

For Long Clawson Dairy, managers and shareholders were keen to buy out Millway as they were interested in building their market share. Taking over a competitor would give them an advantage in the market. This would be a good thing for Long Clawson's workforce, who would enjoy the prospect of more work and greater job security. The take-over should lead to higher sales and, potentially, higher profits. This could lead to higher **dividends** for shareholders.

However, workers at Hartington were to lose their jobs and so were angry at the decision. The impact on the local community could be significant. The workers at the Hartington Creamery tend to live locally and spend their income locally. Other businesses are likely to suffer when the creamery closes. The government was also concerned that the takeover would reduce competition in the market and would be bad for customers.

The point here is that different stakeholders have different viewpoints (perspectives) about the same issue. Conflicts of interest exist. In other words, what is good for one group might be bad for another group.

Conflicts of interest

A conflict of interest exists when different groups want different things.

The decision taken by Long Clawson has a positive impact on shareholders if the take-over leads to higher profits and dividends. However, what is clearly good news for the shareholders is not equally good for all groups. Workers at Hartington will lose their jobs. Customers will potentially lose a favourite product. The interests of different stakeholders are not the same.

The **stakeholder model** is increasingly used by businesses when making important decisions. This involves taking into consideration the views of all interested groups when making decisions, rather than only those of the shareholders. The belief is that conflict between groups can be reduced if the stakeholder model is used.

Different stakeholders - different power

In 2008 the price of gas for UK households rose significantly. This caused many problems for some customers of British Gas and other suppliers. Poorer families, such as pensioners and the unemployed, found their gas bills increasing by 35%. At the same time, the company's profits increased massively, to over £1 billion. In September 2008 the Chairman of British Gas was awarded a £1 million bonus, taking his total salary to £2.8 million for the year. This angered many groups, who felt that large pay awards for executives and managers were inappropriate at the same time as customers were having to pay higher bills.

In both the case of Long Clawson and British Gas there are examples of stakeholders with different amounts of influence. The managers at Long Clawson were in a position to make decisions about the future of workers at the Hartington Creamery. Workers were virtually helpless to protect their jobs. In the case of British Gas, decisions by managers to increase gas prices affected millions of customers. These customers had little influence over this decision.

Source: adapted from http://www.derbyshiretimes.co.uk/peak/Creamery-deal-monopoly-fear.4594256.jp, http://www.dailymail.co.uk/news/article-1053375/1m-pay-rise-way-boss-British-Gas-16-million-customers-face-huge-rises.html

Watch Out!

Dont confuse shareholders and stakeholders. They are not the same thing.

Employees of gas companies and users of gas are stakeholders in gas companies

3 Do all stakeholders have the same perspective?

Test yourself

1. Which of the following is **not** an example of a stakeholder of Royal Bank of Scotland (RBS)? Select **one** answer.

    A Saver at RBS
    B Shareholder of RBS
    C RBS mortgage-holder
    D None of the above

2. UK train operators announced that fares would rise sharply in January 2009. On some routes fares would rise by 11%, well above the rate of inflation. These increases were introduced to fund improvements in rail services. Passenger groups were angry at the decision and insisted the government step in to prevent the increases. A conflict of interest between stakeholder groups existed. The train operators clearly were in a stronger position than passengers.
    Passengers would lose out from the fare increase, but which stakeholder group would be **most likely** to benefit directly from fare increases? Select **one** answer.

    A Government
    B Shareholders of train operators
    C Employees of train operators
    D Owners of shops and cafes in train stations

3. Penwatch Engineering Ltd makes precision components for the car industry. Managers have researched investment into a new piece of machinery which will replace 10 workers and which will increase productivity by 40%. As a result, profit margins will rise and the firm can become more competitive. Which **one** of the following represents the most likely source of a conflict of interest between stakeholders of the business? Select **one** answer.

    A Shareholders and managers of the business
    B The supplier of the machine and customers
    C Shareholders and customers
    D Workers and management

Over to you

Jonaston, a private sector financial business, has announced plans to close its London call centre with the loss of 200 jobs. Some jobs would be moved to the company's remaining UK call centre in Bristol, but the majority would be relocated to India. A spokesperson for the business explained that the decision was essential if the company was to remain competitive. The decision would enable costs to be reduced. Workers were angry at the decision. Many would face redundancy.

1. Which **one** of the following is the **most accurate** definition of a stakeholder? Select **one** answer. (1)
   A Anyone who owns shares in a business
   B Any group which work within a business, such as workers and managers
   C Any group which has an interest in the performance of a business
   D Any group concerned with how a business affects the environment
2. Identify **two** stakeholder groups which might be affected by Jonaston's decision to relocate to India. (2)
3. Explain how **one** of the groups identified in Question 2 will be affected. (3)
4. 'Workers were angry at the decision.' To what extent should Jonaston take into account the views of workers when making decisions like this? (6)

ResultsPlus
Build Better Answers

Tilezone is a roofing company. Recently it has seen orders shrink. Shareholders think that offering services which it has not offered before, such as plumbing and rewiring, can help to increase sales and profits. It also wants to reduce the time it takes to complete projects. Employees in the business are worried about how this might affect them.

(i) Identify **one** source of conflict between employees and shareholders in the business.
(ii) Explain how that conflict might affect employees. (3)

🟥 **Basic** Identifies one source of conflict, such as the offering of new services (1).

🟠 **Good** Identifies one source of conflict and states how this might affect the employees. For example, 'A source of conflict could be that the business wants to offer new services. Employees may need to do jobs that they are not used to doing.' (2)

🔺 **Excellent** Identifies one source of conflict and explains how this might affect the employees. For example, 'A source of conflict could be that the business wants to offer new services. Employees may need to do jobs that they are not used to doing. Some will not have the skills required and may need retraining, whilst others without skills may be made redundant. Some employees may lack motivation and feel under greater strain than they were under before the changes.' (4)

4 Are there any hidden costs or benefits?

Case Study

Brayce Ltd, a pottery business in Birmingham, had enjoyed a successful year. Profits had risen impressively and the business was in the process of an ambitious expansion programme. To reward the workforce for their efforts, director Rob Brayce laid on a lavish party at his Staffordshire home. All 130 staff, with partners, were invited and were treated to a luxury party, ending with an impressive firework display. The fireworks alone cost £9,000. The event was a tremendous success for all concerned, although some local residents were unhappy at the level of traffic which flooded into the village. The noise of the fireworks also led some residents to complain. Additionally, the waste created from the party had to be collected by local council workers. On the other hand, the firework display was watched by many locals who were not invited to the party. A nearby pub saw an increase in trade as locals came to take advantage of the garden which had excellent views of the display.

Objectives

- To understand that choice involves decision-making that affects more than just those immediately involved in the decision.
- To understand that there can be positive benefits and negative costs to others of decision-making.
- To define positive externalities and give examples.
- To dfine negative externalities and give examples.
- To understand how externalities can affect different stakeholder groups.
- To identify real life examples of positive and negative externalities and their impact on different stakeholder groups.

edexcel key terms

Third party – a group or an individual that is not directly involved in a decision/action.

Externalities – the effects of an economic decision on individuals and groups outside who are not directly involved in the decision.

Negative externalities – those costs arising from business activity which are paid by people or organisations outside the firm.

Who is affected by decision-making?

In the example above, the decision by Rob Brayce had effects on lots of different people. The staff of his business were directly affected by his decision. They were part of the reason why he made the decision. It was their hard work and dedication that had helped the company do so well.

However, there were also many other people and groups who had nothing to do with Brayce Ltd who were affected by Rob's decision to hold the party. These people and groups are called **third party** groups. Many decisions that are taken affect a far wider range of people than just those directly involved. To understand the true cost or benefit of a decision, the effect on third parties has to be taken into account. In some cases, decisions can be taken that have positive effects on third parties whilst in other cases there can be negative effects on these individuals and groups.

The above case study illustrates this important economic concept which is called **externalities**. These are the effects of an economic decision on individuals and groups outside who are not directly involved in the decision (third parties).

Negative externalities Negative externalities are those costs from a decision which other people have to bear. The costs are 'external' to the decision. In the example above, the party has effects on the local community. The local council needed to pay for the 'clean up'. The money spent on this clean up could have been spent on other things. The road congestion imposed a cost on local residents. For example, journeys took longer than they usually did, costing more in terms of fuel and time. Finally, some residents were unhappy at the noise from the party. They had to suffer this inconvenience.

The point in all of the above examples is that the 'costs' imposed on these groups were paid for by the local residents - **not** by Rob Brayce or his guests. These costs would be regarded as negative externalities.

4 Are there any hidden costs or benefits?

Positive externalities **Positive externalities** are those benefits received by third parties outside the decision, but for which no payment is made. Think about the local residents who were able to watch the firework display. Did they pay for this display? No - they enjoyed it free of charge. In addition, the landlord of the nearby pub saw a jump in sales as a result of the number of additional people who had come to the village to enjoy the fireworks. The landlord was not involved in the decision to host the party but gained some benefit from that decision.

Different externalities can affect stakeholder groups in different ways. Tables 1 and 2 show how different stakeholder groups can be affected - both positively and negatively - by the actions of other groups.

Table 1 – Examples of negative externalities and their effects

- Water pollution by businesses causes lower catches for businesses and people employed in the fishing industry. Their incomes are reduced as a result.
- Increased car ownership leads to greater emissions of greenhouse gases which speeds up the process of global warming.
- A new bypass is built to reduce traffic congestion in a town centre. This road cuts through an ancient woodland landscape. The views of local residents are spoiled by this road and house values fall as a result.
- A local takeaway leads to large amounts of litter in the surrounding area. Residents find litter in their gardens and need to spend time cleaning up the mess. The local council needs to spend money each week cleaning up the litter.

ResultsPlus Watch Out!

Externalities do **not** have to be money costs. Local residents may be inconvenienced by the noise of a local factory. This is a cost to them even though they do not physically pay this cost.

Table 2 – Examples of positive externalities and their effects

- A local authority spends money improving a local community by providing landscaped gardens. The effect is to increase the value of houses in the area. Homeowners benefit by the actions of the local authority.
- A display of Christmas lights and decorations in a town centre generates lots of extra trade for local businesses as consumers are attracted to visit the display.
- An individual having a 'flu jab' reduces the risk of other people catching influenza.
- Government investment in the West Coast main railway line leads to less congestion on roads as commuters are encouraged to use the train. Drivers who continue to use the roads will benefit, as less congestion means journey times are shorter.

edexcel key terms

Positive externalities – those benefits arising from business activity which are experienced by people or organisations outside the firm. The firm receives no payment for the benefits received.

4 Are there any hidden costs or benefits?

Why are externalities important?

Businesses need to take into account the externalities they produce when they are making decisions. If a business increases its output as a result of a large new order it needs to take account of internal factors. These will include whether it has the capacity to meet the order, does it have the workers, and so on. However, it will also need to take into account the impact on people outside the business. Will the extra work increase the noise for local residents? Will emissions increase as output rises?

The importance of externalities is closely linked to the information on the stakeholder model in section 3. Businesses are increasingly under pressure to consider not only the impact of their operations on their internal stakeholders, but also their external ones as well. The positive and negative externalities they create are increasingly part of their consideration when making decisions.

Over to you

In 2008 a beach in Ceredigion in Wales was polluted by heating oil after a nearby company was found to have a leaking tank. Specialist pollution experts placed barriers across a local stream which was carrying oil to the beach. The clean up operation proved to be very expensive and would have to be paid for by local taxpayers. Local businesses were worried that the pollution could result in a fall in tourism.

Source: adapted from
http://news.bbc.co.uk/1/hi/wales/mid/7689404.stm

1. Identify **one** negative externality from the following caused by the leaking oil tank. Select **one** answer. (1)
   A The cost of repairing the leaking tank
   B The loss in profit for the company with the leaking tank
   C The cost of the clean up operation for local taxpayers
   D The damage to the reputation of the company
2. State **two** other negative externalities for the local community. (2)
3. Explain **one** impact of the oil spill on local tourist attractions. (3)

Test yourself

1. Identify **one** negative externality resulting from rising car use in the UK.

   A The development of new models by car producers
   B Increased congestion on UK roads
   C An increased demand for fuel
   D A rise in the use of public transport

2. Identify **one** positive externality which will result from the opening of a new supermarket in a town. The supermarket is the largest in the local area, employing over 100 staff. The supermarket has built several new roads in the area to improve access.

   A Lower prices for local residents
   B Access to a wider range of products
   C Quicker journey times for drivers in the area
   D More employment for local people

3. An entrepreneur intends to set up a new garage on waste land opposite a housing estate. Which **one** of the following is **not** an example of negative externalities the business might produce?

   A Greater congestion stemming from customers at the business
   B Profits made by the new business
   C Higher house prices due to the improvement of waste ground
   D Noise made by the new business

4 Are there any hidden costs or benefits?

Build Better Answers

(a) Explain **one** possible effect on businesses of an increase in road traffic in a small town. (3)

Think: What effect will an increase in traffic have on a small town? How might this affect business in the town or others out of the town that deal with businesses in the town?

🟥 **Basic** Mentions one factor (i.e. increased road congestion) but offers no explanation or an incorrect explanation. (1)

🟠 **Good** Identifies one factor and offers some explanation that shows how it might affect businesses. The explanation offers a basic link to show the effect. A basic link would be 'an increase in traffic congestion could result in late deliveries to local businesses, causing disruption to those businesses.' (2)

🔺 **Excellent** Identifies one factor and offers an explanation that shows how it might lead to a cash flow problem. The explanation offers up to 2 basic links to show the effect. For example, 'an increase in traffic congestion could result in late deliveries to local businesses, leading to disruption to work, which could increase costs and result in a possible reduction in profit.' (3)

Know Zone: Topic 5.1
How can I start to think like an economist?

In this topic you have learned about: opportunity cost and the idea of trade-off, how decisions taken by individuals, businesses and governments involve making sacrifices, pricing and its importance in business decision-making, how consumers can respond to changes in price for different types of product, considering the idea of price sensitivity, different types of stakeholder and examples of the conflicts of interest that can exist between these different groups and externalities - positive and negative - in real-world situations, considering how these effects influence different stakeholder groups.

You should know…

- ☐ A trade off exists when the selection of one choice results in the loss of the benefits that could have been gained from another choice.
- ☐ Opportunity cost involves the sacrifice of the benefits of the next most desired alternative when making a particular choice
- ☐ Examples of opportunity cost from your own experience and from the economic world.
- ☐ Demand is the amount of product a consumer would like to buy and is able to buy at a given price over a period of time.
- ☐ Price sensitivity measures how much demand for a product changes when price changes. If the price for a product increased significantly but demand did not change in response to this increase, the demand is described as price insensitive.
- ☐ If a change in price leads to a large change in demand then the product is said to be price sensitive.
- ☐ Stakeholders are groups with an interest in a business. They can be internal or external to the business.
- ☐ Conflicts of interest can exist between stakeholders. This is where different groups want different outcomes.
- ☐ Stakeholder groups often do not have equal power or influence. Some stakeholders have more power than others and can therefore influence decision-making more directly.
- ☐ Negative externalities exist when a decision imposes costs on other stakeholder groups. Importantly, the cost imposed is not paid by the business, organisation or Individual who made the decision, but by groups outside - so called 'third parties'. The cost is said to be 'external' to the decision maker.
- ☐ Positive externalities exist when groups outside enjoy the benefits of a decision but do not have to pay for these benefits.

Support activity

- Keep a diary for a week showing what trade-offs you have had to make. Briefly explain the trade-off and why you chose what you did.
- Make a list of all the stakeholders in your own school. Colour code the list, using one colour to identify internal stakeholders and another colour to identify external stakeholders.
- From your lists of stakeholders, identify three examples where a conflict of interest might exist. Briefly explain each example.

Stretch activity

- Think of products which your household buys in a typical week/month. Draw a straight line with 'Price insensitive' written at one end and 'Price sensitive' written at the other.
  Price sensitive ---------------------------------- Price insensitive
- Think about whether the products/services that your household buys are price sensitive or price insensitive and which are most and least price sensitive and place them on your scale. For example, you may find that petrol/diesel purchases are price insensitive - if the price of fuel increases significantly over the next month, your household spending on this is unlikely to fall much.
- Compare the products which you have identified as being price sensitive and price insensitive. Are there any common features of the goods you have identified in each case? Try to identify three 'rules' to explain why the demand for these products have different price sensitivities.

ResultsPlus
Maximise your marks

(a) In 2008 Tesco opened a new supermarket in Hemsworth, West Yorkshire. This store was situated next to the town's existing supermarket, the Co-op. The new supermarket created jobs for local people. Some local residents felt that Hemsworth needed a major supermarket like Tesco. There were some downsides, however. Traffic levels increased significantly in the town centre, with lengthy delays for vehicles travelling through the town. The employees at the Co-op were worried that they might lose their jobs if the arrival of Tesco took custom away from their store. Some local traders felt that they would be put out of business by the opening of another supermarket.

(a) (i) Identify **one** negative externality that might have been caused by Tesco. (1)

(ii) Explain what Tesco could do to reduce the effects of this negative externality. (3)

Student answer

(a) (i) A negative externality is where a business like Tesco causes bad things for other people.

Examiner comment

🟥 A few things are wrong here. First, the student spends too long on the answer. The question is worth 1 mark and therefore does not require a sentence. One or two words will be enough to get the mark. Second, the actual example gives a definition of negative externalities and does not identify one negative externality so does not answer the question. This response shows a basic understanding of the concept, but as it does not answer the question it will not earn the mark.

Build a better answer

🔺 The student should not have repeated the part of the sentence, 'A negative externality is...'. Get to the point. A student who states, 'More congestion' will earn one mark.

(ii) Tesco could provide a free local bus service for customers who want to use its supermarket. This will reduce the number of people travelling there by car and will reduce the congestion in the town centre. Other people will therefore suffer less.

🟠 A good answer that confirms understanding of negative externality - the 'cost' imposed on other groups by lengthy journey times - by identifying a realistic and practical strategy that could be used by Tesco.

🔺 The answer is fine in itself. However, one improvement could be made by making sure the response makes use of appropriate business and economics terminology. In this example the student refers to, 'other people'. Instead, reference could have been made to **stakeholders** or third parties - in this case local residents who are being affected by increased traffic levels.

Practice Exam Questions

Alex Elwell runs a small independent garage and petrol station on the edge of the Peak District in Derbyshire. As the only garage selling petrol and diesel in the local area, his business provides an important product for local people. When making pricing decisions Alex does not really have to take into account the price competitors charge, as his main competitor is a supermarket 15 miles away. However, he does have a loyal customer base and tries hard to provide a friendly service and a reasonable price. The cost for which he buys the fuel from his supplier is the main factor in influencing the price he charges. Alex has found that customers are not particularly price sensitive, as the following data show.

Price per litre (petrol)	Average daily quantity sold (litres)	Total revenue
70p	10,000	£7,000
80p	9,900	(i)
100p	(ii)	£9,800

(a) What are the **two** missing values (i) and (ii) from the table? (2)

(b) The table shows that as price increases, the revenue received by the business increases. This does not, however, mean that the business will make more profit.
(i) Define the term 'Revenue'. (2)
(ii) Define the term 'Profit'. (2)

(c) Alex is in a strong position when it comes to pricing. When the price he charges increases his sales do not fall significantly. As the owner he can be said to be in a stronger position than other stakeholder groups, such as his customers. To what extent should Alex try to keep his prices as high as possible? (6)

Topic 5.2: Risk or certainty?

Topic overview
This topic looks at how the success of business can be measured, the factors that can cause business failure, including the importance of cash flow, the problems faced by an economy, including inflation and unemployment, how changes in exchange rates affect a business's exports and imports and the extent to which Government can solve economic and social problems.

Case study

When James Leach was made redundant from his job as an insurance broker for a large City firm, he decided to pursue his dream of running his own business. In 2001, his new business, Tubs, started trading. Specialising in hot tubs and swim spas, Tubs was the first specialist supplier in the north of England. James started the business with £20,000 he had received as a redundancy payment.

The main supplier for Tubs was a specialist manufacturer in France with an excellent reputation for high quality products. Tubs quickly became established as the main supplier in the market. Revenue increased by 500% over an 18 month period, as people flocked to buy the latest 'must have' accessory. Profit increased significantly and enabled the business to expand its workforce from 5 to 28, with two new stores opening within two years. Of all sales of hot tubs in the north of England, Tubs had 35% of the market, which was a huge market share for such a new business. For a number of years the business grew rapidly and seemed to be destined for a bright future.

Then things began to go wrong. Two rival businesses entered the market, tempted by the profits that were possible. One of these rivals was a national chain which had used a national TV advertising campaign. This business was able to offer free delivery and installation, which Tubs could not. Tubs' costs increased when the exchange rate of the pound against the euro fell. When the business started £1 was worth around €1.60, but by the end of 2007 this had fallen to around €1.35. This meant that the costs of imports from France increased. Also, the price of oil increased during the same period, which meant that delivery costs increased. This cost had to be passed on in the form of higher prices for customers.

Another factor which affected Tubs was the increase in interest rates which the Bank of England had introduced. Over the period 2003-2007 interest rates increased steadily from 3.50% to 5.75%. This meant that households with mortgages had less money to spend on luxuries such as hot tubs.

These factors led to a gradual decline in the quantity demanded of Tubs' products. Sales began to fall and James had to reduce the size of the workforce. By 2008 the business was sold to a competitor, leaving James to think of another idea.

'We were a real success in the early days', states James. 'We had identified a market niche and supplied this with a quality product. However, we didn't pay enough attention to our competitors, who developed a better product. We didn't see the risk'.

1. 'We were a real success in the early days.' What evidence from the case study suggests that the business was, indeed, a success?
2. Identify two factors which appeared to cause Tubs to lose competitiveness.
3. Outline the effect that the change in the exchange rate had on Tubs' business.
4. Discuss two possible effects of higher interest rates on a business such as Tubs.

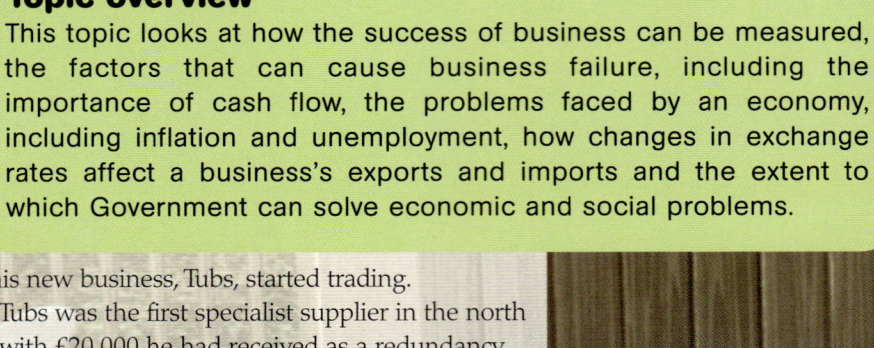

Topic 5.2 Risk or certainty?

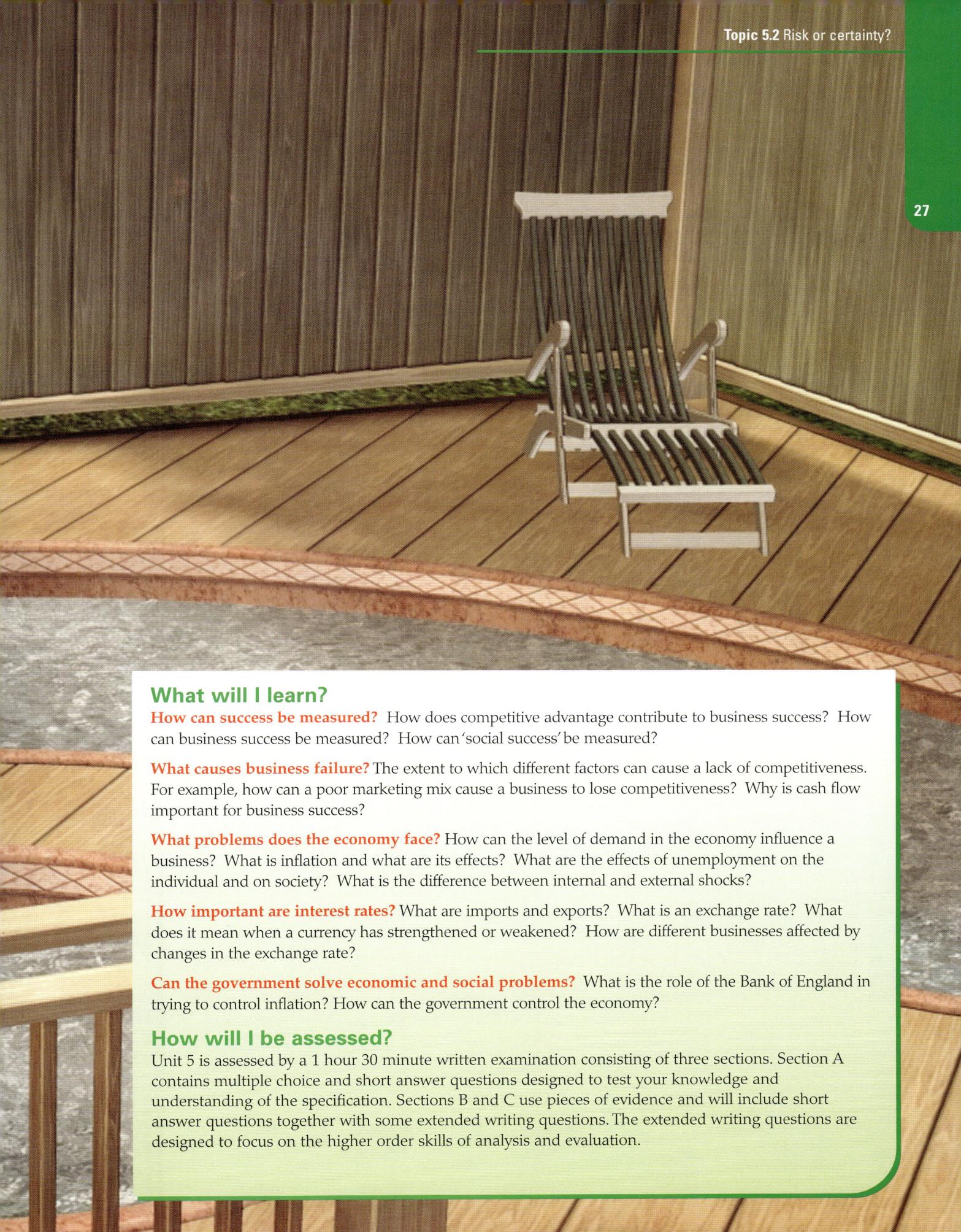

What will I learn?

How can success be measured? How does competitive advantage contribute to business success? How can business success be measured? How can 'social success' be measured?

What causes business failure? The extent to which different factors can cause a lack of competitiveness. For example, how can a poor marketing mix cause a business to lose competitiveness? Why is cash flow important for business success?

What problems does the economy face? How can the level of demand in the economy influence a business? What is inflation and what are its effects? What are the effects of unemployment on the individual and on society? What is the difference between internal and external shocks?

How important are interest rates? What are imports and exports? What is an exchange rate? What does it mean when a currency has strengthened or weakened? How are different businesses affected by changes in the exchange rate?

Can the government solve economic and social problems? What is the role of the Bank of England in trying to control inflation? How can the government control the economy?

How will I be assessed?

Unit 5 is assessed by a 1 hour 30 minute written examination consisting of three sections. Section A contains multiple choice and short answer questions designed to test your knowledge and understanding of the specification. Sections B and C use pieces of evidence and will include short answer questions together with some extended writing questions. The extended writing questions are designed to focus on the higher order skills of analysis and evaluation.

5 How can success be measured?

Case Study

Success - based on quality Trevor Dakin had the idea for a new restaurant in Wickersley, South Yorkshire. In 2007 Vasco was opened. Trevor's intention was to base the business on quality. Vasco employs a top chef with a good reputation. The business has been a great success since it opened. Sales and profit have increased steadily. The restaurant is regularly fully booked and it is necessary to book in advance to secure a table. The business has built a very strong reputation in a short period of time.
Source: Vasco.

Success - based on price Aldi is a low-price supermarket which has expanded in the UK over recent years Sales in 2008 increased by 25%, to £2 billion. The low price chain increased its number of stores from 416 to 457 during 2008. Aldi's success in 2008 has been associated with a recession in the UK. With unemployment rising and confidence low, consumers looked at supermarkets that provided lower prices when buying their regular purchases.
Source: adapted from http://www.freshplaza.com/news_detail.asp?id=36510

Objectives
- To appreciate that competitiveness and competitive advantage contribute to business success.
- To recognise different ways in which business success can be measured.
- To understand the idea of 'social success' – corporate social responsibility.
- To evaluate business performance using business concepts.

edexcel key terms

Profits – the rewards for risk-taking. Profit is the difference between the amount of revenue earned by a firm and the total costs of producing the goods and services the business sells.

Market share – the quantity sold by a business as a percentage of total sales in a market.

Measuring success

Business success can be measured in many different ways. However, to measure success in any field there has to be a benchmark; something to measure success by. For Vasco success meant building a strong customer base and to do this 'quality' was very important. Aldi could measure its success by a large increase in sales during 2008, which led to higher **profits** and enabled the expansion plans of the business to be put into effect. Businesses are often interested in quantitative measures of success, such as sales revenue and profit.

Profit is clearly important for a business. Profit is the reward for enterprise and the owners of businesses for the investment they have made. In general terms profit is found by deducting costs from sales revenue. Higher profits are one indication that a business is successful. Remember, however, that when considering profit it is important to use measures such as profit margin to build an accurate picture of the performance of the business. A profit of £1 million may sound impressive, but if sales in this business were £100 million then this would look far from successful. Indeed, this indicates a profit margin of 1%.

Revenue is the money a business receives from its sales. In general terms the higher the revenue the more successful the business. However, revenue alone cannot be used as a true indicator of business success.

Market share

Market share is an important way for some businesses to measure their performance. Market share is the quantity sold by a business as a percentage of total sales for the product over a given period of time.

The market for mobile phones is very **competitive**. To be successful businesses need to have a **competitive advantage** over rivals. In 2008 the estimated sales of new mobile phones in the UK was over 24 million. This market was dominated by a few producers, with Nokia and Sony-Ericsson between them supplying over 60% of the market as shown in Figure 1. It was Nokia, however, that dominated. Its market share increased from 30% in 2006 to 43% in 2008 as shown in Figure 2. Sony-Ericsson's market share fell from 28% to 18% over the same period. One reason for this success was Nokia's investment in developing new phones, such as the N96.

A large market share is viewed as an indicator of success. It means that customers are choosing the business's products rather than those of competitors.

Social success

Traditional methods of measuring success, such as those listed above, are of course important. However, of growing importance is the idea of '**social success**', which involves how businesses perform in terms of their social, environmental and ethical responsibility. This takes into account the stakeholder model when considering business success. A business may be extremely successful in terms of its financial performance, but be less so when its 'social performance' is taken into account.

To illustrate, consider the example of a clothing retailer that announces profits have increased to 100 million. At the same time the business is found to be using suppliers in the UK who were paying their workers below the minimum wage and who were working in dangerous conditions, and foreign suppliers who paid their workers 4p an hour. So is this business a success? On the one hand, yes. It is making a profit and is therefore ensuring a return for shareholders. However, if we are to take into account the views of all stakeholder groups then the answer is not so clear. The workers who are being paid less than the national minimum wage, and who have to put up with poor working conditions, may have a different opinion from the shareholders.

Most business activity has an effect in some way on society as a whole, whether it be through pollution, waste, packaging, greenhouse gases, using cheap labour and so on. A business's actions have an impact on society. Many larger firms now produce a Corporate Social Responsibility (CSR) report, along with their financial accounts. This gives details of the costs of their activities on society and the environment, and the measures that they are taking to try and reduce those costs.

ResultsPlus Watch Out!

Revenue and profit are not the same thing. Similarly, rising revenue does not necessarily mean a business will be making more profit. This will depend on what is happening to business costs.

edexcel key terms

Competitiveness – the strength of a business's position in a market measured by market share and profitability. It reflects whether people are prepared to use the business over its rivals.

Competitive advantage – advantages that a business has over its rivals. These advantages help to win it customers. To be really effective the advantages must be difficult to copy (defensible) and unique (distinctive).

Social success – the performance of a business which takes account of social, environmental and ethical factors.

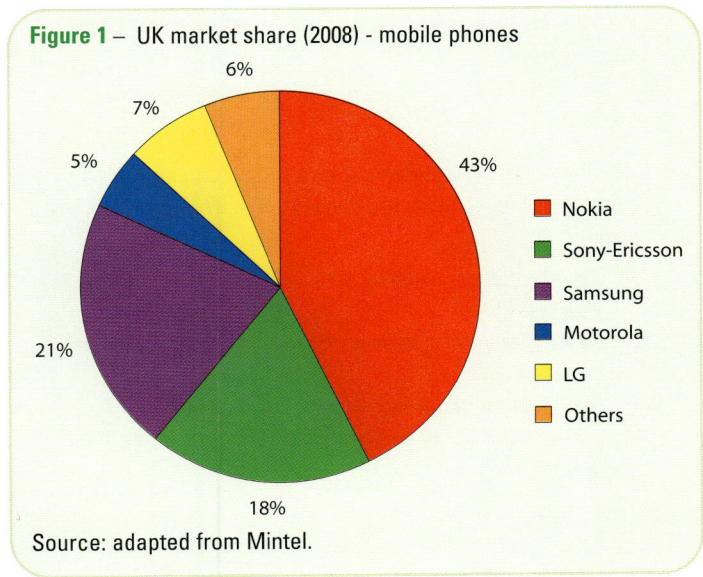

Figure 1 – UK market share (2008) - mobile phones
- Nokia 43%
- Sony-Ericsson 18%
- Samsung 21%
- Motorola 5%
- LG 7%
- Others 6%

Source: adapted from Mintel.

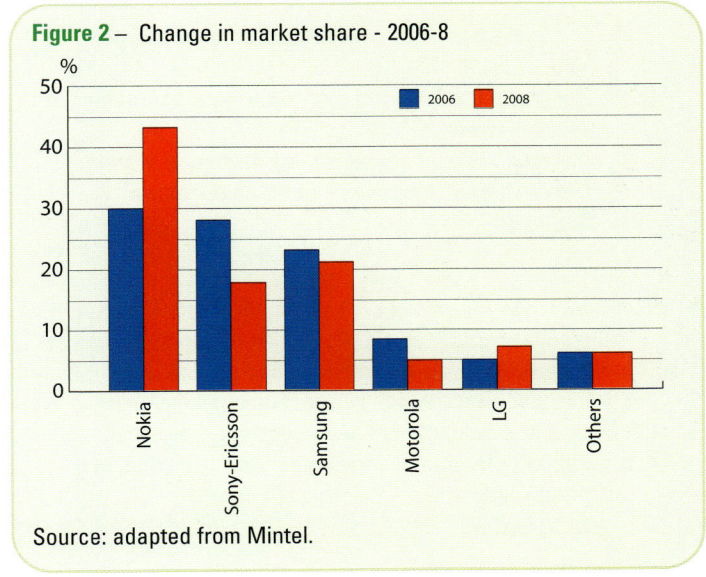

Figure 2 – Change in market share - 2006-8

Source: adapted from Mintel.

Figure 3

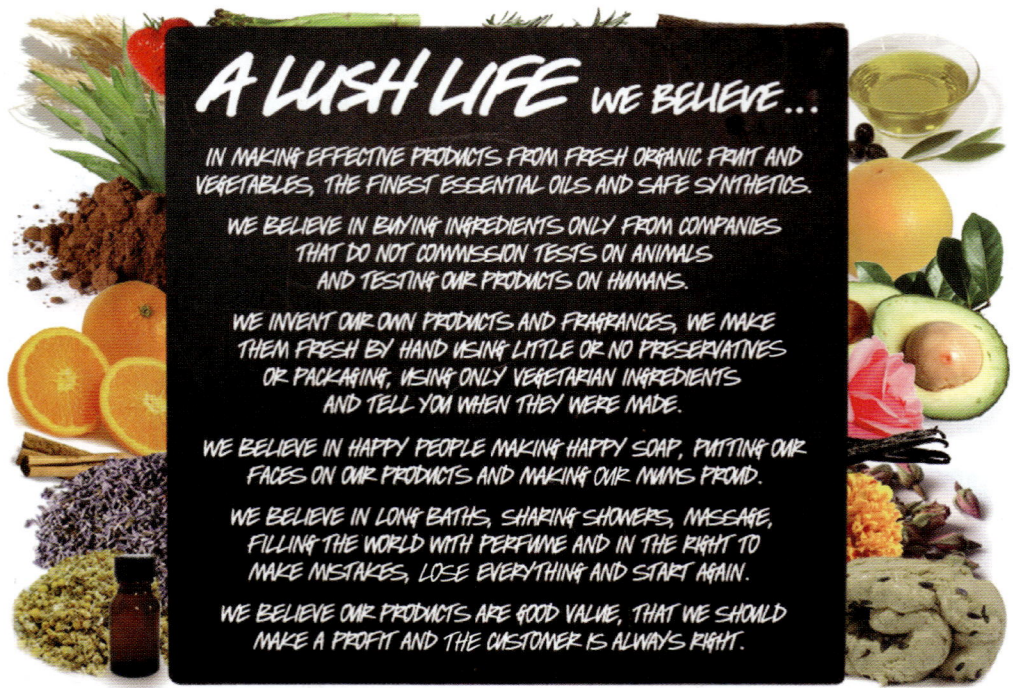

Source: www.lush.co.uk.

For example, Lush is a business which takes its social responsibility seriously. The business produces soaps and cosmetics, but takes care to minimise its impact on the environment by using natural ingredients and by keeping packaging to a minimum. In addition, Lush tries to ensure that it acts as ethically as possible. Business ethics is the sense of moral duty towards all stakeholder groups - trying to do things 'right'. This often involves going beyond what is required by law. For example, Lush does not use ingredients which have been tested on animals.

Environmental awareness

Today people are more aware of the effect that business activities have on the environment. They can see pollution from factories in the sky. They see and hear the news on television about oil spillages. They read articles in

Test yourself

1. Which is the **best** definition of market share? Select **one** answer.

   A The quantity sold by a business as a percentage of total sales in a market
   B The profit of a business expressed as a percentage of its sales revenue
   C The total sales of a product in a particular market.
   D The price of a company's shares on the Stock Exchange

2. In the market for games consoles in the UK, the Nintendo Wii is the market leader. By 2009 over 3.5 million households owned a Wii. But the market is competitive. Sony's PS3 and Microsoft's X-Box 360 are in direct competition with the Wii. Which of the factors mentioned below do you believe to be **most important** for console manufacturers in building a competitive advantage? Select **one** answer.

   A Wide availability of the console
   B Being the lowest priced console on the market
   C Special features of the console, such as game play and graphics
   D Glamorous and enticing advertising campaigns

3. Which of the following would be used by a business as evidence of its social and ethical success? Select **one** answer.

   A An increase in profit by 50% during the latest financial year
   B Development of a new product which is targeted at young people
   C An increase in market share from 12% to 17%
   D Phasing out the use of plastic packaging on its main product line.

newspapers and on the Internet about the effect of waste. Films such as *The Inconvenient Truth*, a documentary by former US vice president Al Gore in 2006, show shocking images of potential damage as a result of climate change.

Stakeholders may regard the effect on the environment by a business as one measure of its success. A business that makes high profits, whilst at the same time causing pollution, may not be regarded as a success by some people. As a result, businesses have been trying to find ways of reducing their impact on the environment. For example, some shops are replacing plastic bags with paper bags. Some supermarkets are encouraging shoppers to buy and use the same plastic supermarket bag rather than single use plastic bags each time they shop. Some shops encourage recycling of printer cartridges.

The CSR tries to show how the business is meeting its responsibility to the environment. This might include switching to the use of more fuel efficient cars or vans, installing energy saving devices in factories and offices, encouraging staff to work from home and reducing packaging and the levels of harmful emissions and waste.

Some people argue that the only reason businesses produce a CSR report is to show customers that they care about the environment. In other words, it is a marketing exercise to try to encourage higher sales and build an image for being a 'good' company.

Over to you

In 2007 Asda, the supermarket chain, was selling school uniforms in its George Range for less than £10 in larger stores. Anti-poverty campaigners suggested that selling at such a low price would only be possible if workers in the developing world were being exploited. Asda insisted that its George uniform was bought only from factories which were regularly audited.

The pressure group, War on Want, doubted this. Its spokesperson, Paul Collins, said, 'It is clearly suspect if it costs less than £10. Time and again, Asda's goods have been found to be made using cheap labour.' The year before, a War on Want report on Bangladeshi factories that made George at Asda clothing found workers were paid only 5p an hour and worked up to 80 hours a week. It also found that factories had poor safety records. 'Factory owners are under great pressure to drive down costs in order to keep contracts with Asda', Mr Collins argued.

Source: adapted from http://www.guardian.co.uk/environment/2007/may/30/supermarkets.schools

1. Identify **one** method which a supermarket chain might use to increase its market share. (1)
2. Explain how the method you have identified in Question 1 could help the business to increase its market share. (3)
3. Identify **two** methods by which a supermarket chain could improve its ethical performance. For each reason, analyse how this would benefit the business. (8)

ResultsPlus
Exam Question Report

1 (d) Identify **two** factors that might affect the competitiveness of a business. (2) (June 2007)

How students answered

Few students (6%) scored poorly (0) on this question. These answers failed to identify any factors correctly.

Some students (23%) gained good marks (1) on this question. These answers may have identified one factor incorrectly or misinterpreted the term competitiveness.

Most students (71%) gained very good marks (2) on this question.
These answers included two correct factors such as price, quality, efficiency, unique selling point (USP), design, skills of the staff and costs of production, for example.

6 What causes business failure?

Case Study

In late 2008, Woolworths, one of the most famous names on the UK high street, went out of business. The shock of this went far and wide. However, there was a number of reasons for the dramatic collapse. For some time Woolworths had struggled with its product range. To many it was unclear what products Woolworths specialised in. Its product range included toys, CDs/DVDs, children's clothing, stationery, confectionery (including its famous 'Pick 'n' Mix'), kitchenware, paint, garden equipment and so on. But for many of these products Woolworths faced lots of competition, and was not regarded as a specialist retailer. Customers had alternatives.

Source: adapted from newspaper articles, 2008.

Objectives

- To know what is meant by business failure.
- To know a range of different reasons why businesses fail.
- To understand what is meant by a lack of competitiveness.
- To understand how the following factors can lead to a loss of competitiveness:
  - poor marketing mix;
  - loss of productivity;
  - increased competition;
  - changing market conditions.
- To define cash flow and recognise how this can lead to business failure.

What is meant by business failure?

Businesses fail when the revenue they earn from sales cannot cover the costs of production. If this happens over a prolonged period of time then the business will become insolvent, where it does not have sufficient funds to pay expenses, and therefore cannot continue to trade. Cash and profit are not the same thing. A business may be profitable in the sense that it is selling its product for a price which is greater than total costs per unit. However, this does not mean that the business is receiving cash at the same time as sales are made. Customers are likely to have credit terms, where payment does not need to be made for 30 or 60 days. The business is likely to still have to pay some costs, such as wages and rents, 'up front'. This might mean that there is more money leaving the business at a point in time than it is receiving in income. When a business cannot pay short-term costs then that business becomes insolvent.

Woolworths failed for a number of reasons. The sort of products sold were also sold by other businesses, often at lower prices, better quality and in the right places. For example, CDs/DVDs are sold by stores such as HMV as well as being available online and in supermarkets, often at lower prices. Children's clothing is available at a range of stores including Matalan and Primark which offer good quality at low prices; Toys R Us and Argos sell toys. Woolworths was selling the type of products which faced stiff competition. In addition, its rivals were more advanced in terms of web-based marketing. Steve Dart, a specialist in marketing, pointed out that:

> 'Many high street retailers are just not switched on to web marketing. Unless potential new customers know the website address, they will typically look for products or services using a search engine such as Google. Woolworths, along with many other major retailers, is nowhere to be seen in searches such as "DVDs" or "children's clothes".'

Source: http://www.netimperative.com/news/2008/november/3rd/guest-comment-could-better-web-marketing-have/view

So a lack of competitiveness in its product ranges and in marketing part of the problem for Woolworths. However, these were not the only reasons for its failure. Another reason for business failure lies in changes in market conditions.

Changes in demand

For a business it is essential that there is a demand for its product. Demand is the amount customers are willing and able to buy at different prices. Where demand for a product falls, the business will see fewer sales and this can lead to insolvency unless steps are taken to address it. Falls in demand can occur for a range of reasons.

- Falling income levels - falling incomes will tend to see demand fall for many goods (but not all).
- Changing tastes and preferences - the demand for white bread has declined as consumers turn to the healthier brown option.
- Fashions - when a product becomes less desirable demand can fall dramatically.
- Advertising - a successful advertising campaign by a rival firm can damage sales. Apple's creative advertising for the iPod is recognised as one of the reasons for its success.
- Competition - if competitors develop better products, then the demand for a firm's product will decline. For example, the introduction of MP3 players led to the decline in sales of CDs and mobile phone manufacturers are constantly introducing new products that make existing ones out of date.

For Woolworths a key factor in its decline was the fact that the UK entered a recession in 2008. During this time unemployment increased dramatically and consumer confidence was damaged. Many High Street firms introduced aggressive sales tactics, slashing prices to attract customers. Many customers thought more carefully about how much they spent in light of the growing risk of unemployment.

The marketing mix - the costs of getting it wrong

The **marketing mix** is crucial for businesses. Getting the right combination of product, price, promotion and place is very important whatever the size of the organisation. A business may have an excellent product, but if the price is too high, or if it distributed in the wrong locations, then failure may lie ahead. Similarly, a business might have an excellent product but if it does not **promote** it effectively, potential customers will not be aware of its existence. Woolworths did not get its marketing mix right. Its product range was too varied; it was not recognised as a specialist supplier of any particular product. In terms of **place**, its lack of Internet presence meant that competitors gained an advantage.

Managing cash flow

Cash flow refers to the money coming into and going out of a business over a period of time. Business do not always receive money at the same time that sales are made. Where customers pay later - using credit - the business may not receive payment for 30 days or even longer. In the meantime the business has had to pay out for costs of materials and wages. If the business has more money going out than coming in, then it will potentially have a cash flow problem. This is also known as a liquidity problem. Figure 1 illustrates how, when a business has more cash flowing out than flowing in, danger is not far away.

Take the example of Alfredo Boreas who had run a family ice cream business for over 30 years. In 2009 the business collapsed. The main reason for the collapse of the business was poor cash flow. The business was profitable, selling high quality ice cream from ice cream vans and direct to retailers. A major order with a regional supermarket seemed to be a good move for 'Boreas'. This required the business to take on 12 extra staff and to extend the manufacturing facilities. Output increased from 2500 litres per week to 12000 litres. However, when the supermarket chain informed Alfredo that they were extending their credit period

Cash is not the same as profit. A profitable business may still face cash flow problems.

edexcel key terms

Marketing mix – the combination of product, promotion, place and price that is designed by a business to achieve its aims. This is also known as the '4Ps'.

Cash flow – the money coming into and going out of a business over a period of time. This refers to the inflows and outflows of money.

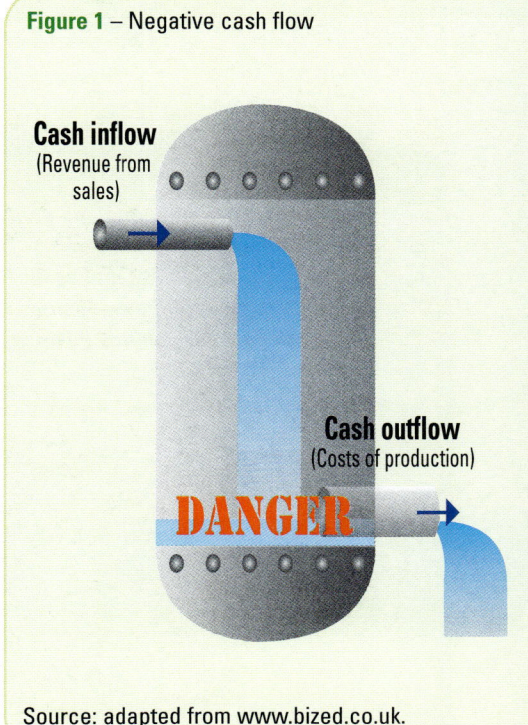

Figure 1 – Negative cash flow

Source: adapted from www.bized.co.uk.

6 What causes business failure?

from 30 days to 90 days, the cash flow problems began. The business found that it struggled to have enough cash to pay day-to-day expenses. The wet summer of 2008 meant that sales in this key part of the year were also much lower than expected. The bank was initially helpful, providing an overdraft facility which provided short-term cash. However, the business eventually became insolvent. Poor cash flow caused the business to fail.

Productivity matters

Productivity measures of the output per worker or machine in a period of time. This is closely linked to the efficiency of a business. If productivity is high then the average cost of producing each unit of output will be lower. For example, two workers are employed to pack cauliflowers into boxes for shipment and get paid £60 per day. Worker A packs 600 cauliflowers a day whereas Worker B packs 400 per day. Worker A is more productive. The **average cost** of each cauliflower s/he packs is 10p whereas the average cost of each cauliflower for worker B is 15p. A low average cost means that a business can charge a lower price for its product or is able to increase its profit margin. This can be a source of competitive advantage for some businesses.

If productivity falls then a business can face problems. This might occur if new firms enter the market and are more efficient. They may have better equipment or purpose built premises which help their workers to be more productive. It may be that firms from abroad who have cheaper wages are more productive and therefore more competitive. If a firm cannot maintain productivity with its competitors then it may be forced to close down.

edexcel key terms

Productivity – the measure of the output per worker or machine per period of time.

Average cost – the cost of producing each unit of output. This is calculated by dividing total cost by the amount produced (output).

Test yourself

1. Which of the following is **not** part of the marketing mix?

   A Price
   B Packaging
   C Promotion
   D Place

   Select **one** answer.

2. Which of the following is the **best** definition of cash flow? Select one answer.

   A The money coming into and going out of a business over a period of time
   B The profit a business makes during the financial year
   C The amount of money a business pays to its suppliers
   D The amount of cash in a business

3. Emily Sanderson was an established florist based in Stamford, Lincolnshire. The business was struggling to survive due to cash flow problems and the level of competition. Its customers were generally in the hotel trade, and were offered credit terms of 60 days. Suppliers were paid within seven days. Which of the following would be the **best** strategy for the business to solve its cash flow problem? Select **one** answer.

   A Increase the credit period for customers
   B Reduce the credit period for customers
   C Reduce the time in which suppliers were paid
   D Increase price to generate more cash inflow

6 What causes business failure?

Over to you

In January 2009 luxury goods company Burberry announced that it was closing its factory in Rotherham with the loss of 290 jobs. The business indicated that the decision was taken in order to reduce costs by £50 million. This was necessary as demand for its products had been affected by the global recession, and by increased competition. Workers at the factory were angry that they were given no notice of the decision.

Burberry has a strong reputation as a fashionable brand. Its clothing range is expensive and is worn by celebrities and models, such as Kate Moss.

Source: adapted from www.timesonline.co.uk.

1. Which of the following might be a source of competitive advantage for a clothing company like Burberry?

   A Available widely in supermarkets
   B Fashionable
   C Cheap prices
   D Advertised widely on TV

   Select **one** answer. (1)

2. State **three** possible reasons for the fall in demand of products for a business like Burberry. (3)

3. (i) Identify **one** method which Burberry might use to increase demand for its products. (1)
   (ii) Explain how this method might increase demand for Burberry products. (3)

ResultsPlus
Build Better Answers

Which of the following is **most likely** to lead to the failure of a local café? Select **one** answer. (1)

A The success of an advertising campaign by the café
B A rise in incomes of customers
C A new café takes 80% of the market
D The sudden change in consumers' tastes

Answer C

Technique guide: There is a number of choices available.

Think: What is business failure? What leads to business failure?

Then: Consider each alternative.

A is incorrect as a successful advertising campaign is likely to lead to more customers and greater sales, rather than business failure. ■

B is likely to lead to more sales as people have more to spend. ■

This leaves C and D.

D could result in a rise or fall in sales. If tastes change to take aways or making food at home, the café may lose customers. If tastes change so that more people eat out, the café might gain customers. ■

This leaves C as the correct answer. A café that was faced by a new business that took 80% of the market is likely to find it difficult to be successful when competing for 20% of the market with other cafés and may go out of business as a result. ▲

7 What problems does the economy face?

Case Study

In November 2008 BMW, the maker of the massively successful Mini (pictured right), decided to close its Oxford factory for four weeks. Workers would still receive their basic pay, but could not earn production bonuses. BMW chose to close the factory rather than make workers redundant. The reason for the close down was that demand for the Mini fell by 40% in September 2008. In early 2009 the business announced a further three shut down following a 29% fall in sales in December. There simply was not enough demand for the car. The business decided that it had to slow down production.

The problem was not only felt by BMW. Car producers in the UK and abroad found that sales were falling. This was due to the global recession which had caused unemployment to increase and spending to fall. For many households a new car was well down their list of priorities. This caused the reduction in demand which had a major impact on businesses like BMW and their workers.

Source: adapted from http://www.thisisoxfordshire.co.uk/news/4047823.BMW__New_Mini_shutdown_at_Oxford_plant

Objectives

- To define inflation in terms of the consumer price index (CPI).
- To understand the causes and effects of inflation.
- To recognise how the changing level of demand in an economy can influence the performance of a business.
- To examine the costs of unemployment.
- To know what is meant by internal and external shocks and give examples of each.

edexcel key terms

Consumer confidence – a measure of the extent to which consumers are prepared to spend money.

Changing demand

The level of demand refers to the amount of spending that takes place in the economy. This spending can be by individuals, businesses and governments. The total level of demand in an economy will have a significant effect on business performance. The level of economic activity refers to the amount of buying and selling that goes on over a period of time. Each day we all engage in some form of economic activity. Every time people buy a newspaper, an ice-cream and the weekly shopping, or put petrol into a car, they contribute to economic activity and the overall level of demand.

The level of demand in an economy can be affected by many factors.

- The level of economic activity - this can rise or fall depending on the amount of buying and selling that takes place in an economy.
- Interest rates - these affect demand in a number of ways. First, if interest rates are high then the cost of borrowing money will be higher. This may put off people who are thinking of taking out a loan. This is particularly important for so-called 'big ticket items', such as cars. Second, households with a mortgage are affected by changes in interest rates. If interest rates change then mortgage repayments tend to change in a similar direction. This means that families may have more or less disposable income which may affect how much they spend. This will have an effect on demand in the economy.
- Consumer confidence - this is a measure of how prepared consumers are to spend money. **Consumer confidence** is affected by current and future possible events. If unemployment is rising consumer confidence may fall as people feel their own jobs may be under threat. In times when the economy is doing well, people may be prepared to spend money on holidays, new furniture, house extensions, new cars and so on - items that would be considered 'luxuries'.

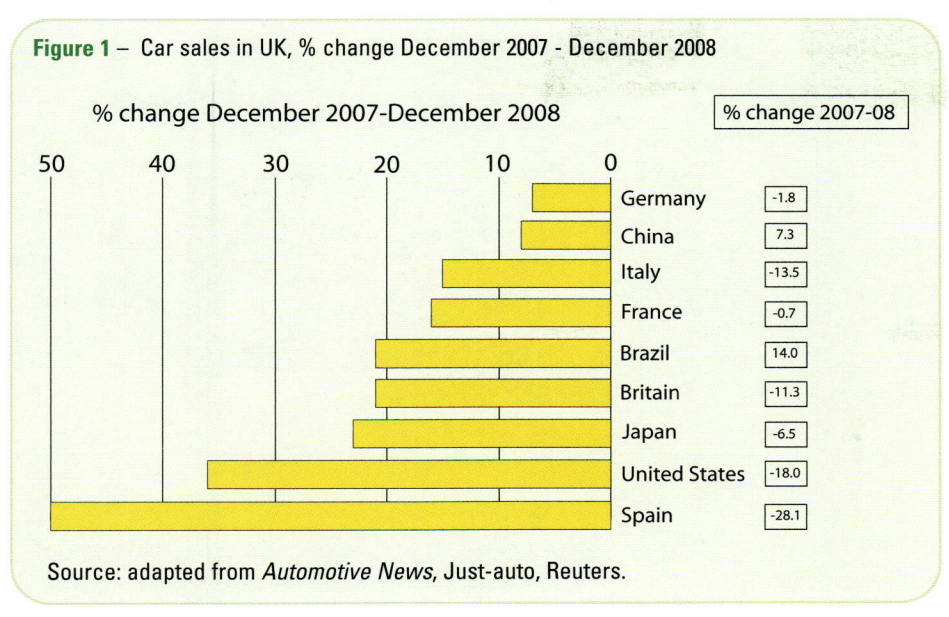

Figure 1 – Car sales in UK, % change December 2007 - December 2008

% change December 2007-December 2008

Country	% change 2007-08
Germany	-1.8
China	7.3
Italy	-13.5
France	-0.7
Brazil	14.0
Britain	-11.3
Japan	-6.5
United States	-18.0
Spain	-28.1

Source: adapted from *Automotive News*, Just-auto, Reuters.

- Demand by foreign consumers - in the case of the Mini, it was not only the demand by UK consumers which had fallen. Demand in other countries had also fallen. The fact that a business sells its products in another country does not mean it is not affected by changes in those countries. Demand is demand, wherever it occurs.

Inflation

Inflation measures the change in the average level of prices in an economy. Prices of goods and services rise and fall over a period of time. A measure is taken of the average change in prices over time to give the rate of inflation. If prices are rising quickly it can be very damaging for an economy. The reason is that price rises create uncertainty; it becomes difficult for businesses to know what prices it will have to pay for supplies, what prices its competitors will charge, what prices to agree contracts at and so on. Uncertainty breeds a lack of confidence. If price rises are not kept under control then the situation can become very unstable.

To consider how rising inflation can get out of hand, consider the case of Zimbabwe. In 2009 Zimbabwe's inflation reached 231,000,000 %. In other words, if a loaf of bread was product priced at one Zimbabwean dollar in January 2008, the price would have risen to 230 million Zimbabwean dollars one year later. This is an example of hyperinflation - an extremely rare phenomenon. Prices have risen so fast in Zimbabwe that paper money ceases to have any value. In January 2009 the government issued a 100 trillion dollar note - that's 100 with 12 zeros. However, a Z$100 trillion note can be used to buy very little - the price of even basic goods like bread is priced in trillions too.

The rate of inflation in the UK is measured by the Consumer Price Index (CPI). This is calculated by comparing the price of a 'typical basket of goods' in one time period to the price of the same 'basket' in another time period. The basket of goods is made up of goods and services that households buy on a weekly and monthly basis and is compiled by the Office for National Statistics. Meat, beans, petrol, insurance, hair gel, DVDs, university tuition fees, furniture, clothes, leisure activities, hotel prices are amongst the 650 representative items in the basket of goods. Price comparisons are taken from 150 areas of the country and around 120,000 separate prices are collected to make up the survey. Inflation exists when the basket of goods costs more than it did in the previous time period. For example, if the cost was originally £200, but increased to £210 one year later, then the CPI would be 5% (£10 ÷ £200 x 100). This represents an increase in the **cost of living**.

ResultsPlus Watch Out!

The best way to remember the difference between internal and external shocks is to think of where they start. A recession in Germany may well affect UK exporters, but it started in another country. In other words, it is an external shock.

edexcel key terms

Inflation – an increase in the general price level. This is measured by the Consumer Price Index (CPI).

Cost of living – a measure of the average cost of basic necessities, such as food, housing and clothing.

7 What problems does the economy face?

Figure 2 – Oil prices

Brent Crude, Price ($), August 07 to June 09, ranging from about 70 rising to a peak near 140 then falling to around 40.

Source: adapted from http://investing.thisismoney.co.uk/companyresearch/100815/Brent_Crude/company_charts.html

Figure 3 – UK inflation - 2007-8

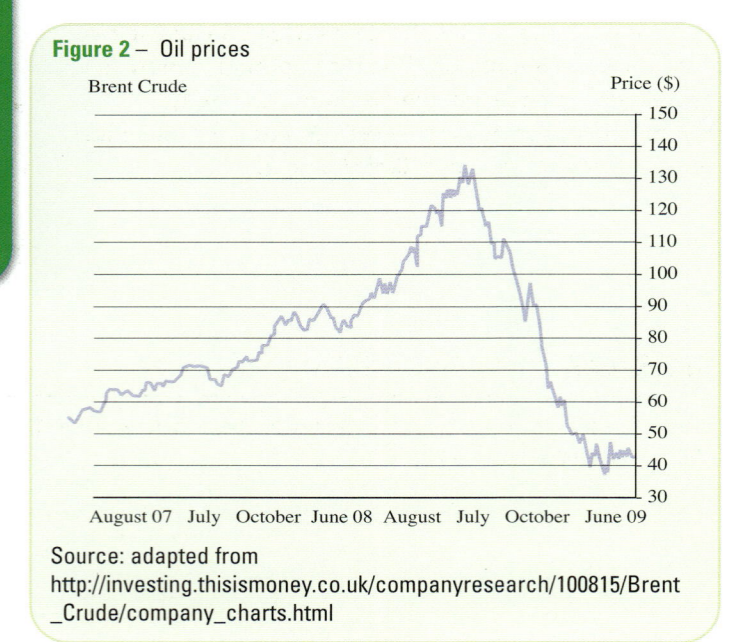

Components: Electricity, gas and other fuels; Food and non-alcoholic beverages; Vehicle fuels and lubricants; Other; CPI (per cent). Percentage points from 2006 to 08.

Source: adapted from http://www.bankofengland.co.uk/publications/inflationreport/ir08nov4.pdf

The CPI shows how fast prices are changing. If prices rose by 5% in year X but by 3% in the next year, prices have **not fallen**. The **rate** at which they have risen has slowed down but prices, on average, are still 3% higher than they were in year X. This distinction is very important.

Inflation can be caused by a number of factors.
- A rise in the cost of production for businesses may be passed on to the consumer as higher prices. The rise might be caused by:
  - rising prices for key raw materials, such as oil, copper, wheat, rice, etc.;
  - higher wage costs;
  - increases in the process paid for imported goods.
- A rise in the level of demand in the economy - especially when supply is not able to keep up. This might be caused by:
  - rising wage levels;
  - increased consumer confidence.

How far prices rise depends on the rate at which demand increases in the economy. It also depends on how easy it is for businesses to pass on higher costs of production and how well they are able to meet the rising demand. In Zimbabwe, for example, the demand for basics such as bread and water is very high but the country is simply not capable of producing enough and so prices have risen very fast. In the UK, the number of people wanting to buy houses and flats in the early part of the 2000s rose quickly but the number of houses available to buy did not rise as quickly and so the average price of a house rose significantly.

If the rate of inflation increases, people come to expect that prices will continue to rise and try to get higher wages to maintain their standard of living. If businesses pay these higher wage costs then they may have to increase prices to maintain their profit levels and a **wage-price spiral** can begin. If not checked the spiral can get out of control.

An important factor relating to the cause of inflation, therefore, is the **expectations** of consumers and businesses.

During 2008 the world price of oil increased dramatically, reaching a peak of $147 per barrel. Many UK businesses rely on oil as part of their production process and the rising price of oil meant their costs of production rose. For example, delivery costs increased as vans and trucks which used petrol and diesel became more expensive to run. This forced businesses to put up prices for goods and services to their customers. Similarly, for many households the price of oil affected their costs as the price of oil influences the price of petrol and diesel. For the first time, the price of unleaded petrol went above £1 per litre. In addition to this, the price of gas and electricity also rose significantly and food prices were also rising because of a shortage of supply of basic items like wheat. The combination of all these things caused average prices to rise and businesses and families found that their cost of living increased. Inflation increased from around 2% in 2005 to over 5% by 2008.

These sort of dramatic changes are referred to as a shock. If the change occurs due to a factor outside the country, then this is an **external shock**. The oil price is set on the world market for oil. It changes due to changes in the demand and supply of oil. Other external shocks can occur due to a fall in the exchange rate, which makes imports more expensive. **Internal shocks** are unanticipated changes in demand and costs in an economy arising from within the country. For example, a successful harvest for wheat will

edexcel key terms

External shock – an unanticipated change in demand or inflation caused by factors beyond the control of the country, for example, a rise in oil prices or a fall in the exchange rate.

Internal shock – an unanticipated change in demand or inflation caused by factors within the country.

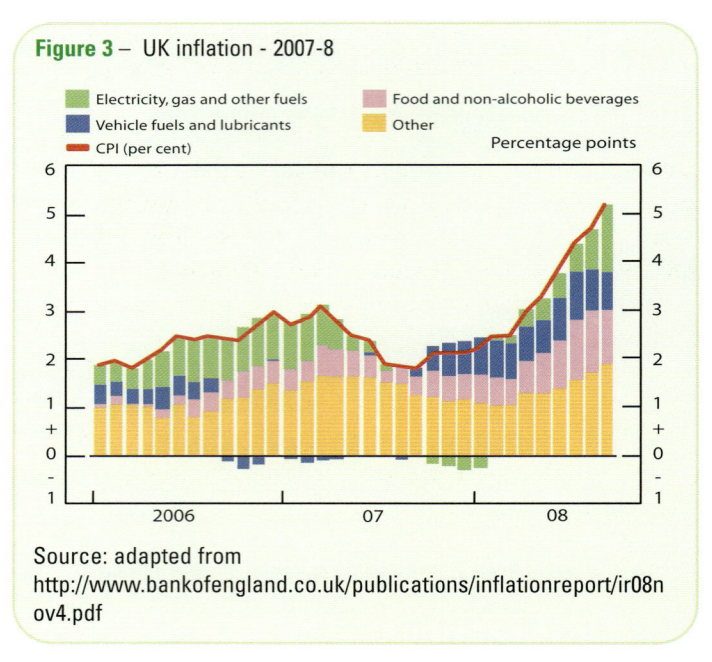

tend to force the price of wheat down. This will be a benefit for consumers and businesses that use wheat.

The problem of unemployment

Another problem an economy can face is that of unemployment. Unemployment is said to exist when people who want to find work cannot do so. The government has two measures of unemployment.
- Claimant Count - a monthly count of those claiming unemployment benefits such as Jobseeker's Allowance.
- Labour Force Survey - a measure based on a monthly survey of over 63,000 households to identify who is seeking work. This measure takes into account people who are seeking work but do not qualify for Jobseeker's Allowance.

For our purposes the distinction between the above two measures is not important. What is important is how unemployment can affect the economy. Certainly unemployment has negative effects or 'costs' for individuals and for society, as shown in Table 1 and 2.

edexcel key terms

Tax revenue – money received by the Government from people and businesses paying their taxes.

Table 1 – Costs to an individual of unemployment

- A lower level of income than would be received if they were employed. This will often affect the individual's and family's standard of living.
- Loss of self-esteem - individuals may feel depressed and worthless during periods of unemployment.
- Losing skills - being out of work for a period of time may result in a loss of skills. This may make it even more difficult for people to find work in the future. It may become part of a cycle of unemployment.
- Family break-up - during periods of unemployment divorce rates increase.

Table 2 – Costs to society of unemployment

- Taxes - during periods of high unemployment the Government will receive less **tax revenue**. This may affect spending plans in other areas. For example, during the recession of 2008-9, the government scrapped plans to spend over £5 billion widening 220 miles of motorway.
- Benefits - when people are made unemployed they generally qualify for state benefits. The main support in this area is Jobseeker's Allowance, but there are also housing benefits, income supports, and so on. These benefits represent a significant cost for government. If Government income is falling, but spending is rising, it may have to borrow more to cover its spending.
- Crime - this tends to rise in recession. When incomes fall some people become tempted to turn to crime.
- Impact on other businesses - as unemployment rises there may well be an impact on other businesses, as with the case of the Mini at the start of this chapter.

7 What problems does the economy face?

Test yourself

1. Unemployment can have significant costs for a society. Below is a list of impacts. What of the following is a **possible effect** on the UK of high levels of unemployment? Select **one** answer.

   A Rising inflation due to higher levels of spending
   B Increased consumer confidence
   C Higher levels of taxation to fund higher benefit payments
   D Lower crime rates

2. Inflation is an increase in the:

   A size of the economy
   B level of demand in an economy
   C level of supply in an economy
   D level of prices in an economy

   Select **one** answer.

3. Which of the following is an example of an internal shock to the UK? Select **one** answer.

   A A prolonged increase in house prices, resulting in UK consumers having more confidence
   B A 50% increase in the world price of oil
   C A recession in Germany causes the demand for goods from the UK to fall
   D A lower exchange rate of the pound causes increased demand for UK goods by US consumers

ResultsPlus Exam Question Report

4 (b) Analyse **two** possible effects of a high unemployment rate on a country. (6) (June 2007)

How students answered

Some students (47%) scored poorly (0-2) on this question. These answers may simply have identified two effects for 2 marks, such as a burden on the health system, a rise in crime, a fall in tax revenue for the government, a need to raise taxes or lost output to the economy.

Some students (44%) gained good marks (3-4) on this question. These answers would have taken into account that the question says 'analyse' and developed each effect that is identified. For example, for one effect, 'High unemployment can make taxes higher. This is because the government has to pay benefits to the unemployed.'

Few students (9%) gained good marks (5-6) on this question. These answers would have analysed two possible effects in detail. For example, for one effect, 'High unemployment can make taxes higher. This is because the government has to pay benefits to the unemployed. people who are in jobs will therefore have to pay more to support those who are not in work. These people will take home less income.'

7 What problems does the economy face?

Over to you

In 2008 the rate of inflation in countries with the euro as their currency - the eurozone - reached a record high. In August of that year inflation hit 4.1%, well above the target set by the European Central Bank (ECB).

The increase in inflation was caused by two factors. First, food prices had risen and were causing higher general prices. Second, the oil price had increased dramatically during 2008. This affected costs of many businesses. These costs were passed on to consumers in the form of higher prices.

The ECB indicated that steps would be taken to control the effects of this external shock to prices.

Source: adapted from:
http://www.independent.co.uk/news/business/news/rising-oil-and-food-prices-push-inflation-in-eurozone-to-record-high-882689.html

1. Which of the following is a possible cause of rising inflation in an economy? Select **one** answer. (1)

   A   Increase in interest rates
   B   Lower food prices
   C   Lower demand by consumers
   D   Higher costs of commodities such as oil

2. Explain what is meant by external shock. (3)

3. Explain **one** effect of inflation on an economy. (3)

8 How important are exchange rates?

Case Study

Nonsolovino was opened in November 2008 in Chesterfield, Derbyshire by its owner, Peter Gately. The business imports Italian food and wine from specialist suppliers across Italy. The pound-euro exchange rate is crucial for the business, as it purchases its supplies in euro and then sells them in sterling (pounds). Changes to the exchange rate can affect Nonsolovino directly. In early 2008 £1 could buy around €1.30. For Nonsolovino this meant that a bottle of wine priced at €13 in Italy, would mean Pete had to give up £10 to buy each bottle. The business plan was designed with such an exchange rate in mind. However, throughout 2008 the pound weakened against the euro. This meant that £1 could buy fewer euro and for Nonsolovino this meant that goods in Italy priced in euro now meant it had to give up more pounds to get the same amount of euro. As a result the business needed to decide whether to increase the price it charges UK customers, or accept a lower profit.

Source: information provided by Nonsolovino.

Objectives

- To define the terms imports and exports and give examples of each.
- To understand what an exchange rate is and recognise when a currency has strengthened or weakened.
- To explain the effect of changing exchange rates on import and export prices and how these changes affect businesses.
- To recognise the impact of exchange rate changes on different businesses.

edexcel key terms

Exports – goods and services which are sold to other countries and which lead to payments to the UK.

Imports – goods and services bought from other countries which lead to money going out of the UK.

Exchange rate – the value of one currency in terms of another.

International trade

We live in a global economy. Buying and selling goods and services internationally is taken for granted. Imports are goods and services we buy from abroad for which a payment is made to a foreign business. For example, buying a German car involves a car moving from Germany to the UK, with the payment for the car moving from the UK to Germany.

Exports refer to goods and services sold abroad by a UK business. If a UK business sells wheelie bins to a business in France it will receive a payment.

Imports mean money goes out of the country to pay for the item whereas exports mean money comes into the country in payment. The direction of the payment is important in identifying imports and exports. For example, if a school party goes to New York on a business studies trip, is this an import for the UK or an export? The answer is that it represents an import because the school is buying the tourist services provided by the USA and payments are made to the US.

What is the exchange rate?

An **exchange rate** is the amount of one currency that has to be given up to acquire another currency. An exchange rate of £1 = €1.30 means that an individual or business has to give up £1 to get €1.30 euro. Exchange rates change every day. When the exchange rate changes this can affect different stakeholders in different ways depending on the direction of the change. The terms 'strengthened' and 'weakened' are used when exchange rates change and it is important to understand what is meant when an exchange rate has strengthened or weakened.

What causes the exchange rate to change?

The actual exchange rate of any currency is determined by the buying and selling of foreign currencies on world currency markets. Like anything which is bought and sold, the price of a currency is fixed by the forces of demand and supply.

Currencies are traded on international markets and every day billions of pounds are traded for other currencies. Traders on these markets are specialists and act for clients such as banks and businesses. Banks and businesses will want to buy and sell currencies because:
- they have to pay for UK exports and to invest and save in the UK;
- they have to pay for imports from abroad and to invest and save outside the UK.

Banks and businesses need to have currencies available to satisfy the needs of their customers. For example, a German family wishing to take a holiday in the UK will go to their bank to order pounds so they can pay for goods and services in the UK. They will demand pounds and supply euro.

Nonsolovino, in the example above, requires euro to pay for the wine and other products it buys from its suppliers in Italy. The business will require its bank to buy euro using its pounds so they can pay their Italian suppliers. Nosolovino demands euro and supplies pounds.

Traders on foreign exchange markets spend their day buying and selling currencies. As demand and supply change so do exchange rates. Demand and supply can change for many reasons. For example, if the Bank of England increases the rate of interest in the UK, then the demand for pounds is likely to increase, as foreign investors convert their currency to pounds to save in UK banks which now have higher interest rates. In this example the exchange rate of the pound would increase.

Strengthening exchange rate Exchange rates can be tricky to understand, and come with their own terminology. A key thing to remember is that this section all relates to a UK perspective. If the pound increases in value, it is said to **strengthen**. This means that a pound will buy (be exchanged for) more of a foreign currency. Look at the example in Table 1. In April, one pound could be exchanged for 1.5 euro. In June, the exchange rate is £1 = €2.00. The value of the pound has risen (strengthened) because £1 can now be exchanged for €2 rather than €1.50. It is stronger in the sense that it will buy more of a foreign currency.

Weakening exchange rate The reverse is the case when the pound falls in value; when this happens it is said to **weaken**. In the example in Table 2 the pound has **weakened** against the euro. In June £1 could be exchanged for €2.00. However, in November the change in the exchange rate means that every pound can now only be exchanged for €1.40.

We can see how the change in the exchange rate can affect a business.
Nonsolovino buys 500 bottles of Italian wine each month. The euro price of the wine is €10 per bottle. The total amount that the business has to pay for the wine, therefore is €5,000.

If the exchange rate in April is £1 = €1.50 then Peter will have to give up £3,333 to acquire €5,000 (5,000 ÷ 1.50).

When the exchange rate changes in June to £1 = €2.00, Peter now has to give up £2,500 to get the €5,000 he needs to pay his suppliers. The strengthening exchange rate has benefited him as he now has to give up less pounds to get the same amount of euro. His costs have fallen by around £833 a month.

However, by November the situation has changed again. He now has to give up £3,571.43 to acquire €5,000 to buy his wine (5,000 ÷ 1.40). Compared to June his costs have risen by £1,071.43.

The position for a business which imports goods or services from abroad would be the exact opposite of the above.

ResultsPlus Watch Out!

Always remember that when businesses in different countries trade with one another, they will want payment in their own currency. A business in the UK wanting to buy wine from Italy will need to convert pounds into euro. How many euro they receive for each pound depends on the exchange rate.

Table 1

	April	June
Exchange rate (£ = €)	£1 = €1.50	£1 - €2.00

Table 2

	June	November
Exchange rate (£ = €)	£1 = €2.00	£1 - €1.40

8 How important are exchange rates?

Why is the exchange rate important?

For an importer, such as Nonsolovino, the exchange rate is important because the suppliers in Italy will require payment in euro. To pay these suppliers the business needs to convert - or exchange - pounds for euro. The amount of euro received for each £1 depends on the exchange rate.

How does the exchange rate affect other stakeholder groups?

During 2007 and the first part of 2008 the pound **strengthened** significantly against the dollar. Figure 1 shows that at its peak £1 was worth over $2.

This strengthening of the exchange rate was good news for UK holiday makers who were visiting the USA. Tourists received more dollars for their pounds, making their holiday cheaper than it might have been. It also led to an increase in shopping visits to the USA by UK shoppers keen to grab a bargain. The availability of cheap flights meant that individuals could save lots of money by doing their shopping in New York rather than London. If UK shoppers couldn't manage to actually fly to the USA, then the ability to buy products online meant that they too could take advantage of the strong pound. And there were plenty of bargains to be had.

The following gives an example of how the exchange rate can affect prices for foreign shoppers. A Fender Telecaster guitar was being sold to United States customers for $749.99. When the exchange rate of the pound to the dollar reached £1=$2, then this made the price to UK customers £375. If the pound weakened against the dollar to £1 = $1.50, then the cost of the same guitar to a UK shopper would now be £500. For this reason the exchange rate is an important factor in influencing decisions by consumers and businesses.

Are all businesses affected by changes in exchange rates?

In the examples above, changes in the exchange rate affect the amount people and businesses have to pay for goods. For Nonsolovino, the falling exchange rate of the pound against the euro meant that the cost of importing goods from Italy increased. This has implications for the business in terms of profitability and pricing. For a UK business buying goods from abroad, the weakening pound would have the opposite effect - it would benefit from a weakening pound because it would have to give up less pounds to get the currency it needed.

However, many businesses may not be importers or exporters, and may therefore not be directly affected by any changes in the exchange rate. Bear in mind that such businesses may still be indirectly affected by any changes. A restaurant in York may not import or export anything, but a weakening exchange rate of the pound against other currencies will be likely to mean that foreign tourism to the UK increases. If there are more tourists in York then the restaurant may benefit from increased business.

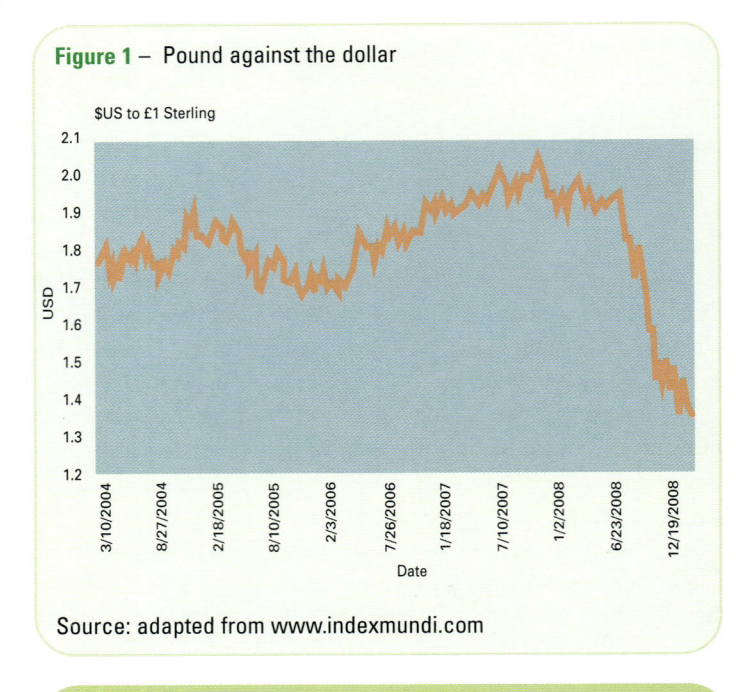

Figure 1 – Pound against the dollar

Source: adapted from www.indexmundi.com

Test yourself

1. Which **one** of the following is an example of an export from the UK? Select **one** answer.

   A A Nissan car produced in Sunderland and sold to a Spanish car dealer
   B A UK student taking a holiday in France
   C A UK manufacturer buying a new ICT system from a German supplier
   D A student buying a pair of jeans on eBay from an American seller

2. The exchange rate between the pound and the euro stands at £1 = €2. How much would a UK business buying cheese from France have to pay if the French price was €40 per pack? Select **one** answer.

   A £10
   B €10
   C £20
   D £40

3. Eleanor Weatherill runs a small business in South Yorkshire selling high quality pens and stationery. The price of a typical fountain pen she sells starts at around £100. Her most expensive pens sell for over £1,000. Since she launched her website in 2005 her online sales had steadily increased. However, during 2008 the strengthening of the pound against the US dollar led to a reduction in sales to customers in the US. Which strategy below would not be appropriate to deal with this situation? Select **one** answer.

   A Increase advertising in US specialist pen magazines
   B Increase the price of pens in pounds
   C Reduce price of pens in pounds
   D. Offer free postage and packaging to US customers

Over to you

How much do 'doggies in the window' cost? Toy retailers have warned that toy prices are likely to rise in 2009. The reason for the prediction is the continued weakness of sterling. Most imports of toys are priced in dollars. A weak pound means that imports cost more money.

This year the dollar/pound exchange rate has weakened by 25 per cent to $1.50. As a result, retailers will be forced to pass on higher import costs to customers.

'Toy retailers' profits will fall and there will be some price increases,' said Gary Grant, managing director of one major retailer.

Source: adapted from *The Observer*, 23.11.2008.

1. Define the term exchange rate. (1)
2. Using an example from the article, state what is meant by a 'weak pound'. (2)
3. Assess the effects of a weak pound on toy retailers in the UK. (8)

ResultsPlus
Build Better Answers

A business in the UK sells 20% of its products to the USA, but imports 70% of its materials from the USA. Assess the effect a strong pound against the dollar might have on its profits. (8)

Answer C and E

Think: What is meant by a strong pound against the dollar? How does a strong pound affect exports? How does it effect imports? What effect do these have on profits?

🟥 **Basic** A limited understanding of how a strong pound against the dollar affects a business. For example, a strong pound can affect competitiveness. Exports may fall, but import costs may also fall for the UK business. (1-2)

🟠 **Good** A clear link is shown between a strong pound and profitability. For example, 'A strong pound against the dollar means that US customers have to pay more dollars for UK goods in pounds. Faced with higher prices, they may reduce spending and exports may fall as a result. On the other hand fewer pounds are now needed to buy US goods in dollars. So the costs of imported materials could fall. Fewer exports can reduce revenue and profits, but lower import prices will increase profits.' (3-5)

🔺 **Excellent** The link between a strong pound and export competitiveness, import prices and profitability will be considered. To gain the highest marks there will be an attempt to say which is bigger. For example, 'A strong pound against the dollar means that US customers have to pay more dollars for UK goods priced in pounds. Exports to the USA will become uncompetitive and suffer a fall in sales. On the other hand fewer pounds are now needed to buy goods priced in dollars. So the costs of imported materials or components could fall. The business may see some falls in export sales, but it depends on how big the changes are. It only exports 20% of its goods to the USA. Sales in the UK and to other countries could be unaffected. Its import costs should fall a great deal as it imports 70% of its materials from the US. Overall its profits should increase as the fall in costs is likely to be greater than the fall in revenue.' (6-8)

9 Can the Government solve economic and social problems?

Case Study

In February 2009 the Bank of England reduced its 'Base Rate' from 1.5% to 1%. This was the lowest rate of interest that the Bank had ever had. Interest rates had been cut dramatically from 5% in 2008. The reason was that the UK was in a serious recession, where economic activity was falling and unemployment was rising.

Source: adapted from http://www.bized.co.uk/cgi-bin/chron/chron.pl?id=3292

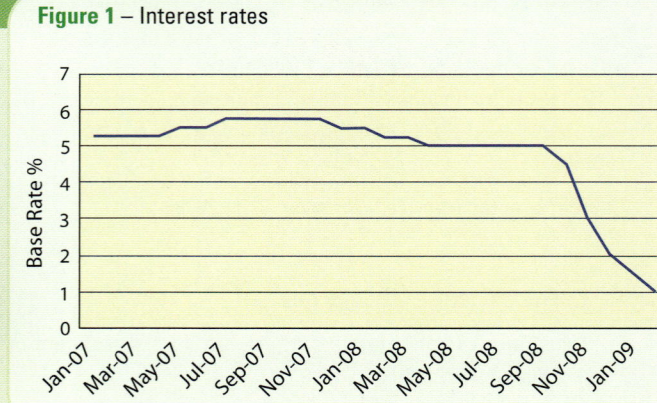

Figure 1 – Interest rates

Objectives

- To explain what interest rates are.
- To understand how the Bank of England uses interest rates to affect the economy.
- To understand how interest rates can affect the level of spending in the economy.
- To know at least five reasons for government spending in the UK.
- To know at least three types of taxation in the UK.
- To evaluate the role of taxation and government spending in dealing with social problems.

edexcel key terms

Interest rate – the cost of borrowing money, or the returns received on savings.

Economic activity – the total amount of buying and selling that takes place in an economy over a period of time.

Monetary policy – the use of changes in interest rates to control inflation.

Fiscal policy – the use of taxation and government spending to achieve government objectives.

Interest rates

The *interest rate* is the price that has to be paid to borrow money. It is also the return received on savings. Individuals borrow money to pay for things such as cars, household equipment, holidays and so on. 80% of households in the UK have a mortgage, a long-term loan for the purpose of buying property. Businesses borrow money to buy new machinery and equipment, or to expand. For all borrowers the rate of interest is important as it influences how much will need to be repaid. It influences how much needs to be repaid each month. Changes in the rate of interest can have a significant effect on the level of *economic activity*. This is the total amount of buying and selling that takes place in an economy over a period of time. The Bank of England sets the Base Rate. This is the rate that they lend to commercial banks like HSBC. The Base Rate determines the level of interest rates charged by banks and other financial Institutions. When the Bank changes interest rates, banks and other financial institutions also change their interest rates. This has an effect on the level of economic activity.

Table 1 summarises how high and low interest rates affect individuals and businesses.

In general terms, higher interest rates tend to slow down the level of economic activity. High levels of spending will lead to inflationary pressure building. Increases in the interest rate will help to reduce ('cool') spending in the economy and thus reduce the rate of inflation. In the example above, as the Bank of England reduces interest rates it will have the effect of stimulating economic activity. Changing interest rates is associated with *monetary policy*.

A taxing problem

The government gave the Bank of England the power to change interest rates in 1997. This effectively meant that the government would not be tempted to use interest rates to stimulate the economy when it might not be the most appropriate tool. However, the Government does have other tools it can use to influence the level of economic activity.

Fiscal policy is the use of taxation and government spending to achieve Government objectives. The Government raises money - tax revenue - from the taxes that people and businesses pay. Workers pay income tax. Businesses pay

Figure 2 – Government spending by function

Total Managed Expenditure: £623 billion

- Other - £62bn
- Debt Interest - £34bn
- Public Order and Safety - £33bn
- Housing and Environment - £24bn
- Industry, Agriculture and Employment - £19bn
- Defence - £36bn
- Education - £83bn
- Transport - £21bn
- Health - £111bn
- Personal Social Services - £27bn
- Social Protections - £173bn

Source: adapted from http://www.hm-treasury.gov.uk/d/pbr08_chapter1_379.p

Figure 3 – Government receipts

Total Receipts: £545 billion

- Other - £73bn
- Council tax - £25bn
- Business rates - £23bn
- VAT - £83bn
- Corporation tax - £45bn
- Excise duties - £42bn
- National Insurance - £98bn
- Income tax - £157bn

Source: adapted from http://www.hm-treasury.gov.uk/d/pbr08_chapter1_379.p

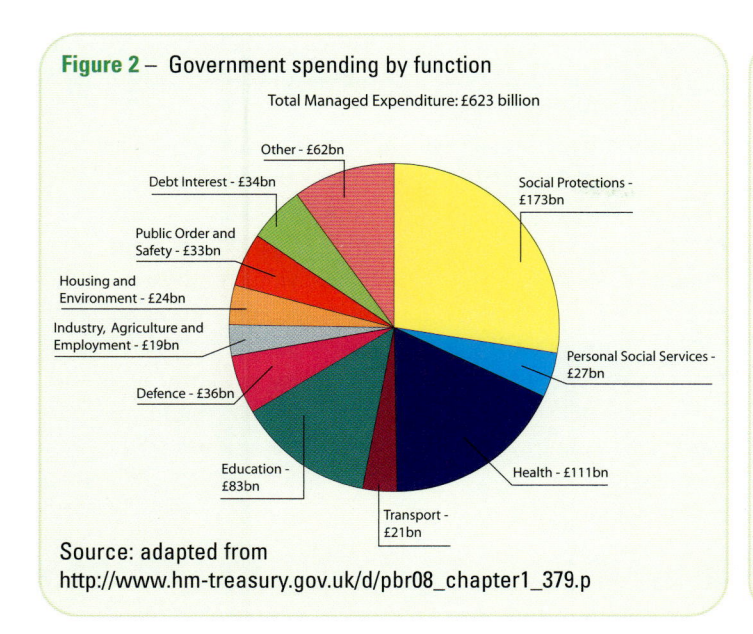

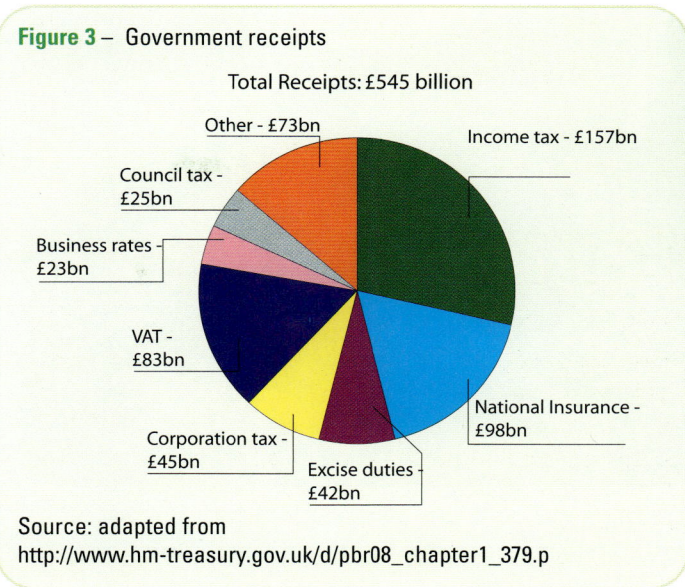

corporation tax on any profits they make. Businesses pay Value Added Tax (VAT) (although it is passed on to consumers) on many goods and services. For the financial year 2008-9, the Government raised £545 billion (see Figure 3). In the same period the Government planned to spend £623 billion. If you are wondering how the Government can spend more than it receives, the answer is rather boring. It borrows the money, in the same way that a household might borrow money to buy a new car if it did not have enough money.

Taxes can be used to influence the level of economic activity. In 2008 the government temporarily reduced the rate of VAT by 2.5% to 15%. This would make goods and services for which VAT was charged cheaper. The Government hoped that cheaper prices would encourage people to spend more and help boost economic activity. For cheaper items the reduction only amounted to pence or a few pounds, but for more expensive items, such as a Tag Heuer watch priced at £10,000, the lucky buyer would have saved over £200.

The level of income tax also influences the economy. In general terms, if taxes are lower then spending will be higher. In the UK the basic rate of income tax is 20%. This is low by historical standards.

Why do we need taxes?

You are possibly wondering, if lower taxes will stimulate economic activity why bother having taxes at all? The answer lies in the fact that the Government spends a lot of money. In Figure 2, we can see that the Government spends around 25% of its entire tax revenue on 'Social Protection'. This is spending on pensions, benefits and other means of support. £111 billion is spent on health, whilst £83 billion is spent on education. We can perhaps agree that these are important services that we expect to be provided. If we need a doctor or hospital treatment, we expect a service free at the point of use; similarly with education. We expect that pensioners will receive an income when they retire, and that people, if they become unemployed, will receive some support from the government.

Social problems

Governments will have economic objectives to achieve such as generating economic growth or keeping inflation under control. Fiscal policy, as we have seen, can be used to help influence the level of economic activity. However, governments also have other objectives they want to achieve and fiscal policy is also used to help achieve these objectives.

Table 1 – The effects of high and low interest rates

High interest rates

Lower spending by individuals - as mortgage payments increase households have less disposable income.

Fewer loans - individuals will tend to be put off by higher interest rates and may delay spending on 'big ticket' items.

Less business investment - many business investments are funded by loans from banks. When interest rates are high businesses tend to put off investment decisions. This reduces the amount of economic activity.

Savings - individuals and businesses are more tempted to save, attracted by the high rates of interest. This reduces the amount of spending in the economy.

Low interest rates

More spending - as mortgage payments fall households have more disposable income and will spend part of this.

Increase in loans - as loans become cheaper individuals can be tempted to take out loans. This leads to higher levels of spending in the economy.

Increased business investment - loans become cheaper and businesses are more tempted to fund expansion.

Savings - as money saved will earn lower returns, individuals and businesses will be encouraged to spend rather than save.

9 Can the Government solve economic and social problems?

Government attempts to solve social problems, such as crime

One of the objectives of governments is to try to solve social problems. These problems include:
- child poverty;
- crime;
- anti-social behaviour;
- binge drinking.

Taxes and spending can be used to address these problems. The UK Government has a stated aim to reduce child poverty. The Labour Government in 1997 set itself a target of reducing child poverty by half by 2010-11 and taking all children out of poverty by 2020. The Government can use taxes to create incentives - for example, to help people get back into work and off benefits - and to support poorer families. It can use its spending to help improve housing, provide better education, support families who need training and parenting help and so on to try and achieve this aim.

Changing habits

So taxes are raised to try to influence the economy, and to provide services which we have come to expect. There is also a third purpose of taxation. Taxes can be used to help change behaviour. Taxes are charged on products which can be viewed as damaging for those consuming them, and for society in general. If taxes are raised then the price of the product or service increases and there is less of an incentive to buy them.

Cigarettes, for example, are extremely damaging to individuals who smoke. They also impose a cost on other taxpayers, because smokers will typically require more health care than non-smokers. This imposes a huge cost on the National Health Service (NHS). The cost of providing health care in 2008-9 was £111 billion. Cigarettes have a very high level of tax imposed on them; typically 80% of the price of a pack is paid in tax. The purpose of the tax is to discourage this type of spending and to help people make the 'right' choices. Taxes are imposed on other products to do the same thing.
- Alcohol - as with smoking, alcohol imposes a massive cost on the NHS as well as on social services and the emergency services.
- Petrol/diesel - private and business vehicles contribute to climate change through emissions of carbon dioxide and other greenhouse gases.

Another major social problem is binge drinking - consuming alcohol in unhealthily large quantities quickly with the intention of getting drunk. Binge drinking causes health problems for the individuals concerned but also involves external costs to society. Drunken behaviour can lead to violence, disorderly behaviour and vandalism and can increase the likelihood of such things as unwanted pregnancies. The emergency services and the health service in many towns and cities are at full stretch on Friday and Saturday nights in particular dealing with people involved or affected by the problem.

One solution that has been put forward is to make alcohol more expensive by raising the tax on it. This will put it out of the reach of some younger people who have limited incomes and also reduce consumption in older people. It has been suggested that this will help to change behaviour and contribute to people drinking more responsibly.

Is taxation effective in solving these problems?

Whilst taxes can help to influence decisions on what people spend their money on, it is worth noting that, despite high taxes over many years, problems still persist. Any observation of a town/city centre, or a typical motorway, during morning or early evening, will confirm that drivers are not being forced onto their bikes, or onto buses/trains, by the high cost of fuel.

In the same way that fuel taxes do not seem to work in achieving their objectives, the same can be applied to alcohol. Alcohol companies argue that they already pay high taxes and that increasing them further would damage their business. The consumption of cigarettes, however, has declined. The proportion of the adult (16+) population who smoke has fallen from 39% in 1980 to 21% in 2007. The duty (tax) on tobacco has changed behaviour but it has also had other effects which might not be desirable. The consumption of cigarettes with duty paid in the UK has fallen from 99 billion in 1990 to 47 billion in 2007. The consumption of cigarettes brought in from abroad which have not paid duty has risen from 3.5 billion to 17.5 billion over the same time period. Taxes can work, but not always perfectly.

ResultsPlus Watch Out!
Remember that the Bank of England's main role is to use interest rates to control inflation **not** the economy. The effect of changes in interest rates will, however, affect the level of economic activity.

Over to you

VAT cut by 2.5% to boost the economy

In November 2008 the government announced that VAT would be temporarily cut from 17.5% to 15%. The intention was to encourage people to spend more. As the economy entered recession, unemployment had started to increase. Businesses were beginning to suffer as people were cutting back spending. The government hoped that businesses would pass on the VAT cut and would reduce their prices to encourage spending.

Pizza chain welcomes VAT cut

Edin Basic, a former manager of Starbucks, set up Firezza, a trendy pizza chain and delivery service in 2001. The business employs 120 people across eight branches and turnover this year will be over £3m. He welcomes the cut in VAT announced by the chancellor on Monday.

However, he does not plan to use the cut in VAT to reduce prices, but instead he plans to use it to increase his profit margins, which have been damaged recently by other government measures, such as the recent increase in the minimum wage rate.

'A few pence off the price of a pizza is not going to make people buy a lot more,' he says, adding that Firezza aims to pass on some of the benefit the business receives through discounts for existing customers and the creation of a loyalty scheme.

Source: adapted from www.ft.com, 24.11.2008.

1. Identify one reason why government imposes taxes on people and businesses. (1)
2. Explain the reason for the reduction in VAT described in the article. (3)
3. The reduction in VAT by the government was intended to increase economic activity. Using the evidence, assess the likely success of this policy. (8)

Test yourself

1. Which of the following is the **best** definition of 'interest rate'? Select **one** answer.

   A The increase in the average price level over a period of time
   B The price of borrowing money and the return on savings
   C The price of one currency compared to another currency
   D How much profit is earned from an investment project

2. Which of the following is not an example of a UK tax? Select **one** answer.

   A Value Added Tax
   B Corporation tax
   C Food tax
   D Income tax

3. Which of the following is not a reason for taxation in the UK? Select **one** answer.

   A To raise money to pay for the NHS
   B To discourage spending on 'harmful' products
   C To support people who are in poverty
   D To pay for imports from foreign countries

ResultsPlus
Build Better Answers

Explain how an increase in the rate of interest by the Bank of England might reduce inflation. (3)

Think: What is meant by an increase in the rate of interest? What is meant by a reduction in inflation? What effect does an increase in interest rates have on groups or individuals? How does this affect prices?

■ **Basic** A simple statement is given such as 'Increasing interest rates reduces spending.' (1)

● **Good** A statement is given with some explanation, for example, 'Increasing interest rates makes borrowing more expensive. Spending falls as a result and firms are less wiling to increase prices.' (2)

▲ **Excellent** A clear indication of how an increase in interest rates might reduce inflation, using linkages and terminology. For example 'An increase in the rate of interest will lead to a fall in spending, since borrowing becomes more expensive. Individuals and businesses are less prepared to borrow money as the cost of borrowing has risen and borrowers have more to pay back. This leads to less demand for goods and services and so firms are reluctant to increase their prices.' (3)

examzone

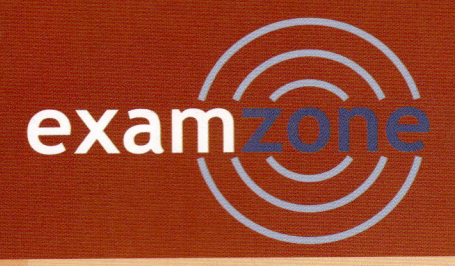

Know Zone: Topic 5.2
Risk or uncertainty?

In this topic you have learned about: what is meant by competitiveness and competitive advantage, and how business can improve both, how success can be measured, using financial as well as wider, 'social' measures, why businesses can become less competitive and what they can do about it, changes in demand, the importance of cash flow to a business, economic activity and inflation, internal and external shocks, what exchange rates are and why they can be important to businesses, the effect of changes in interest rates on economic activity and how the government deals with economic and social problems.

You should know…

- [ ] That competitive advantage exists when a firm appeals to customers more than a rival.
- [ ] Profit is an important measure of success, but profit margin is a better measure.
- [ ] Social success is measured by a business's performance against ethical, environmental and social factors.
- [ ] Business failure can be caused by a change in demand.
- [ ] Demand can fall for many reasons including changes in income, fashions and competition.
- [ ] Getting the marketing mix wrong can lead to business failure.
- [ ] Cash flow involves flows of money into and out of a business.
- [ ] Cash flow and profit are not the same thing.
- [ ] Productivity measures the amount of output per worker or machine per period of time.
- [ ] Rising productivity means lower average costs.
- [ ] Economic activity is the amount of buying and selling that takes place in an economy.
- [ ] Greater spending in an economy can lead to higher inflation.
- [ ] Inflation is associated with higher average prices in an economy and can be controlled by the use of interest rates.
- [ ] The difference between imports and exports.
- [ ] That an exchange rate is the value of one currency in terms of another.
- [ ] How different businesses are affected by exchange rates.
- [ ] What 'the interest rate' is and how it affects economic activity.
- [ ] Methods by which the government can affect the economy.
- [ ] Examples of what the government can do to try to solve social problems.

Support activity

Using a spreadsheet, find out from the Office of National Statistics (ONS) or Biz/ed the interest rate, inflation, unemployment and economic growth rate over the past 12 months. Produce a chart for each and write a short summary of what has happened to these key variables over the last twelve months.

Stretch activity

Use newspapers and Internet resources to build a scrapbook of stories recording examples of business success and business failure. Produce a table to show the reasons for the success and failure.

Article - title/date	Reasons for success	Reasons for failure
Apple to launch latest iPhone *The Times* February 2009	Marketing Mix - Apple is bringing out a new product. This might give the business a competitive advantage.	
RBS announce that 2,300 jobs in the UK are to be cut. *Guardian* February 2009		RBS is making a loss and therefore needs to reduce costs. It will achieve this by lowering labour costs.

ResultsPlus
Maximise your marks

Throughout 2008 unemployment in the UK began to increase. By early 2009 it had exceeded 2 million. This was the highest figure for a number of years.

Unemployment causes many problems for individuals and for society. Individuals may find their income levels fall and their standard of living deteriorates. For a society, government spending on benefits will have to increase; this may mean that spending elsewhere - hospitals, roads, etc. - will have to fall.

(a) Which of the following best describes unemployment? Select **one** answer. (1)

A Where people who want to work are not able to find work
B When prices rise in the economy
C An increase in the number of people working from home
D An increase in government tax levels to pay for unemployment benefits

(b) Identify **two** costs of unemployment for an individual. (2)

(c) Explain **one** cost of unemployment to a society. (3)

Student answer	Examiner comment	Build a better answer
(a) B	This is incorrect. A is the right answer. The candidate has not identified the correct definition.	▲ The student needs to know definitions of key words. This knowledge will enable them to identify suggestions which are clearly incorrect.
(b) More taxes to pay for unemployment benefits. Lower level of income.	● The first suggestion is more linked to society and the Government than to the individual. The second answer is correct. One mark out of two.	▲ Where questions ask you to 'state', 'list' or 'identify' - don't write out full sentences. For this question the following would have received two marks: - Profit - Market share
(c) Unemployment means that some people are not working and therefore the country is not producing enough.	■ A simplistic response which hints at a reduction in GDP. Terminology is lacking. The response generally lacks development, although the candidate shows some understanding.	▲ Try to incorporate the use of key concepts such as opportunity cost. Begin by highlighting the cost. For example, 'Lower output - as people are not in work businesses will produce less and therefore the output of the economy (GDP) will be less. This may mean that incomes in the country begin to fall.'

Practice Exam Questions

Stuart Collins is a photographer specialising in car features and sporting occasions. He has built a reputation as a talented photographer and is employed on a regular basis by magazines such as *Car* and *Evo*. The photography market is very competitive, with individual photographers often seeking to secure contracts by charging lower prices than rivals.

Stuart's competitive advantage lies in the quality of his work, rather than in lower prices. He knows that some competitors will charge much lower than him.

'It is very competitive, but I believe that by offering a quality service and superb images, the demand for my work will continue'.

One problem Stuart faces is cash flow. He has to pay money to undertake a project. If he is contracted to photograph the launch of a new car in Spain, he needs to pay for his own travel before claiming the expenses from the magazine or the car manufacturer. These can take months to be paid.

(a) Which of the following **best** describes the idea of competitive advantage? Select one answer. (1)

A Where a business earns more profit than another business
B A market where lots of companies compete with each other
C Where a business is preferred to rival businesses
D A business charging lower prices than competitors

(b) State **two** possible methods by which Stuart Collins might measure the success of his business (2)

(c) Explain **one** way in which Stuart Collins might improve his cash flow. (3)

Topic 5.3: Big or small?

Topic overview
This topic considers how businesses grow, the reasons why they grow and the benefits and problems that may be generated from growth, the nature of monopoly power and whether monopoly power is good or bad for society and the extent to which large businesses can be controlled through self-regulation or Government intervention.

Case study

A merger occurs when two businesses agree to join together. There are advantages to be gained for businesses when they join together in this way. For example, where offices exist in the same city, the business may be able to close down one to save costs.

In 2008 the bank HBOS merged with rival Lloyds TSB. The merger between two major businesses created a retail giant worth £30 billion. This merger was controversial because of the size of the two banks. HBOS already had a market share of 20% of mortgages in the UK. Lloyds TSB had a market share of 8%. This meant that the new business would have a combined market share of 28%. This was above the maximum market share of 25% which is allowed by the government.

As HBOS and Lloyds TSB often have branches on the same street across the UK, the fear of many customers and workers was that many branches would have to close. It was suggested that as many as 1,000 branches would close, with total job losses up to 40,000.

The government controls the growth of businesses to ensure that they do not become too big. Where a business has a market share of 25%, it is said to be a monopoly. Such large businesses reduce competition. They can charge higher prices, which is a worry for consumers. Monopolies can also provide a poorer service or product than a business which faces lots of competition. The government organisation responsible for investigating instances of the possible abuse of monopoly power is called the Competition Commission.

The government agreed to the merger even though the new combined business had a market share above the 25% limit. The reason for this was that the banking sector was suffering and the merger was the best way to ensure the survival of such important businesses.

Source: adapted from www.timesonline.co.uk.

1. What is a monopoly?
2. Why did HBOS and Lloyds TSB want to join together in a merger?
3. Explain two possible benefits for consumers when lots of competition exists in a market.
4. Discuss (a) one possible effect of the merger of HBOS and Lloyds TSB on customers and (b) one possible effect on shareholders.

Topic 5.3 Big or small?

What will I learn?

How do businesses grow? What is meant by internal growth? How can changing the marketing mix leads to growth? What is external growth? What is the difference between a merger and a take-over?

Why do businesses grow? What is to be gained from growth? What are economies of scale and why do they matter?

Monopoly power - good or bad? What is a monopoly? Are monopolies always bad?

Can big business be controlled? Why does the government want to control big business? What is the Competition Commission? Is self-regulation better than government regulation? What are pressure groups and do they have a role to play?

How will I be assessed?

Unit 5 is assessed by a 1 hour 30 minute written examination consisting of three sections. Section A contains multiple choice and short answer questions designed to test your knowledge and understanding of the specification. Sections B and C use pieces of evidence and will include short answer questions together with some extended writing questions. The extended writing questions are designed to focus on the higher order skills of analysis and evaluation.

10 How do businesses grow?

Case Study

Kennedy Interiors was established in 1998 by David Kennedy. A university degree in fine art had inspired David's interest in interior design. Having completed two small scale projects in the summer after leaving university, David decided to set up as a sole trader. Based in rented small office premises in the centre of York the business quickly grew and David's reputation as one of the top interior designers in the area grew. By 2004 David's order book was extensive, with customers placed on a waiting list of up to 9 months. He realised he needed to expand by employing another designer. New premises were found in Leeds in 2006. By this time the business employed 9 people.

In 2006 L'Oreal, the French cosmetics business, merged with The Body Shop, a British cosmetics company with strong ethical and environmental credentials. The merger was desirable for both businesses. For L'Oreal it was an opportunity to build its ethical image, something which was of growing importance in the cosmetics business. For The Body Shop, joining forces with a global brand would mean expansion into new markets and countries. At the time of the merger L'Oreal had annual sales of £14.5 billion, whilst The Body Shop had sales of £615 million. By joining together the combined business would be much larger. This was an example of external growth - where businesses grow by joining with another business.

Source: adapted from http://ec.europa.eu/competition/mergers/cases/decisions.

Objectives

- To define internal growth and external growth.
- To understand how internal growth can be achieved by changing the marketing mix, innovation and research and development.
- To define merger and give examples.
- To define takeover and give examples.

edexcel key terms

Internal growth – occurs when a business increases in size by selling more of its goods/services without taking over or merging with other businesses.

External growth – where a business grows in size due to merger or takeover.

What is business growth?

The answer to this question is straightforward. A business grows when it sells more goods and services in one time period than a previous period. Growth is often an important objective for businesses, as this is one way to increase profits. Other reasons include the following.

- To increase **market share** - this enables a business to have more control in a market. This can lead to rivals being forced out of business.
- To take advantage of **economies of scale** - larger businesses can achieve lower average costs, which can lead to higher profits.

Whilst growth itself is simple to explain, understanding why growth occurs is slightly more complicated. For our purposes, we will distinguish between **internal growth** and **external growth**.

Internal growth

Internal growth or **organic growth** occurs when the business grows by selling more than it previously did. The additional profit can then be ploughed back into the business to fund further expansion. Kennedy Interiors grew by a process of internal growth. Customers were attracted to the business because of its reputation. The increased sales enabled the business to invest in expansion and new premises. There are various ways that a business can increase sales.

Changing the marketing mix By changing the marketing mix, businesses can achieve growth. Greater use of promotion should increase awareness of the product and encourage more sales. Wider distribution - place - should do likewise. An example is shown in Figure 1.

10 How do businesses grow?

Figure 1

In 2009 Starbucks, the global coffee shop chain, launched an instant coffee. Called Via, the product was a new development for Starbucks, which based its business on providing fresh coffee. Starbucks was keen to enter the market for instant coffee, which was worth $17 billion per year. This was clearly a major market and the business saw the opportunity to increase sales and profits by entering this market. Howard Schultz, the Chief Executive, indicated that the instant coffee market was a 'very significant opportunity' for Starbucks. By changing its product portfolio, Starbucks was aiming to achieve internal growth.

Source: adapted from http://www.ft.com/cms/s/0/500bcd9c-fd5d-11dd-a103-000077b07658.html

ResultsPlus Watch Out!

Creative ideas to increase sales are not only found in very large businesses; a local greengrocer offering a weekly delivery service for seasonal vegetables is an example. A shop introducing a new queuing system to reduce waiting time for customers might be another example.

New product development This involves identifying new products or services that will lead to increased sales for a business. Apple has been very inventive and **innovative** over the past 20 years, producing the first home computer and subsequently developing innovative new computers, such as the iMac and iBook.

Apple has continued to come up with a range of new ideas in its computers. This process often arises from **Research and Development** (R&D), which is the process of creating and designing new products and new methods of production. Some businesses spend vast amounts of money on R&D. For example, Apple spent $185 million in 2008. The purpose of this spending is to find ways of increasing sales, which lead to internal growth.

External growth

A business can grow by simply selling more of its product - however this increase in sales comes about. At the start of this chapter the example of L'Oreal and The Body Shop illustrated how businesses can also grow by joining together. In this example the businesses took part in a **merger**. This is an example of external growth, which occurs when a business grows by joining with another company. In the example above, each business retained its identity.

edexcel key terms

Innovation – the process of transforming an invention into a product that customers will buy. It is the commercial exploitation of an invention.

Research and Development (R&D) – the process of creating and designing new products and new methods of production.

Merger – where two or more firms agree to join together. This is a voluntary agreement and results in the new businesses retaining the identity of both businesses.

Apple has grown by developing innovative new products over many years

External growth can be through merger but could also be through a takeover. In this situation one firm gains control of another firm by buying a sufficient number of its shares. In this situation, the firm taken over may not retain its identity and instead becomes part of the business which took it over. Ryanair, the low cost airline for example, tried to take over Aer Lingus, the national carrier of Ireland. Ryanair owned around 30% of the shares of Aer Lingus in early 2009 and was looking to increase its share ownership to take over the business.

Business acquisitions, both merger and **takeover**, can take place at different stages of the production process or at the same stage of the production process. **Horizontal integration** takes place when acquisition takes place between two businesses at the same stage of the production process. Ford merging with Volkswagen would be an example of horizontal integration. **Backward vertical integration** involves two businesses at different stages of the chain of production joining together, for example, if The Body Shop bought the farms which produced the natural ingredients for its products. **Forward vertical integration** occurs when a business joins with another which is further forward in the chain of production. In 2004 Dairy Farms of Britain, an organisation made up of over 2,000 UK dairy farms, spent £75 million to take over a huge processing facility, meaning it had control of the milk processing stage, as well as the production of the milk. A **conglomerate merger** occurs when two businesses join which have no common business interests. The merger between carmaker General Motors and Electronic Data Systems was an example of conglomerate merger.

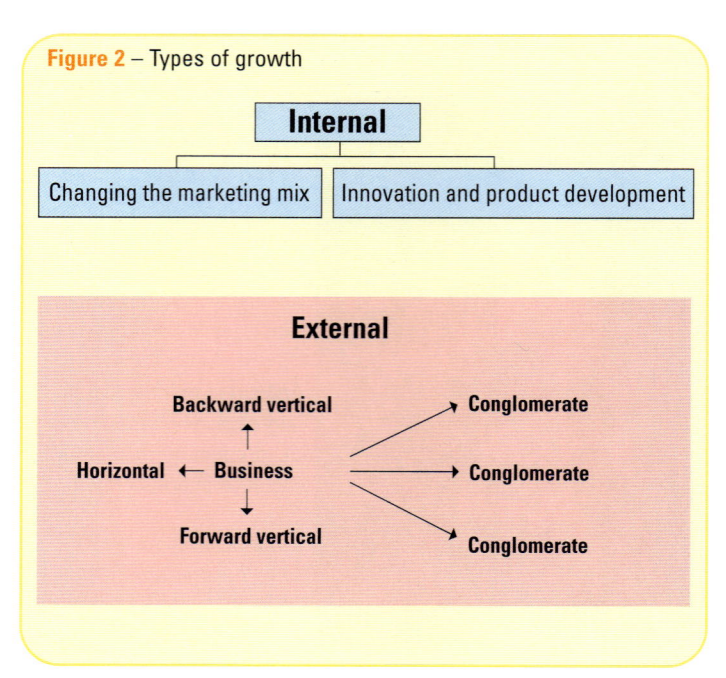

Is external growth always a good thing?

External growth can be a much quicker way for a business to increase its size than internal growth. However, rapid growth can cause problems for the business and for different stakeholder groups. Take-overs and mergers often lead to job losses. Where two businesses which already have Head Offices join together, then costs can be saved by closing facilities which are duplicated. When the European brewer Carlsberg and Heineken took over the UK brewer Scottish and Newcastle (S&N), it did so on the understanding that S&N's Head Office in Edinburgh would be closed with the loss of 500 jobs. Additionally, the combined business may lead to the loss of identity for individual businesses.

Figure 2 – Types of growth

Internal
- Changing the marketing mix
- Innovation and product development

External
- Backward vertical → Conglomerate
- Horizontal ← Business → Conglomerate
- Forward vertical → Conglomerate

ResultsPlus Watch Out!

Internal and external growth are not the same thing. Internal growth occurs when a business increases in size by selling more of its goods/services without taking over or merging with other businesses. External growth is where a business grows in size due to merger or takeover.

edexcel key terms

Takeover – where one business buys another business.

Conglomerate merger – occurs when two businesses join which have no common business interests.

Over to you

The Swedish car producer Saab, which is owned by the American car giant General Motors (GM), is to seek to break away from its parent company after GM threatened to cut support to the company.

GM bought out 50% of Saab in 1990, and the remaining 50% in 2000. This was part of a strategy of external growth designed to increased sales and market power.

GM is experiencing extreme difficulty due to the global decline in car sales, and has asked the US government for $16.6 billion of financial support. GM is to cut 47,000 jobs worldwide.

Saab employs 4,100 workers in Sweden with another 10,000 jobs linked to the business through suppliers and sub-contractors. It fears that unless it breaks away from GM the business could collapse with massive job losses and serious implications for the Swedish economy.

Source: adapted from http://www.telegraph.co.uk/finance/newsbysector/transport/4737085/Saab-seeks-to-break-free-of-GM.html

1. The merger between GM and Saab is an example of which type of integration? Select one answer. (1)
   A Conglomeration
   B Forward vertical integration
   C Backward vertical integration
   D Horizontal integration
2. Explain the difference between internal growth and external growth. (3)
3. Explain one disadvantage of external growth for a business. (3)

Test yourself

1. Which is the definition of merger? Select **one** answer.
   A Where two or more businesses voluntarily join together
   B Where two businesses work together in designing a new product
   C Where one business buys the shares of another company
   D Where one business buys sufficient shares in a business to control it

2. In 2007 travel companies Thomas Cook and MyTravel announced a merger worth £8 billion. Both companies operate mainly as travel agents providing package holidays. What **best** describes this merger? Select **one** answer.
   A Conglomeration
   B Horizontal integration
   C Forward vertical integration
   D Backward vertical integration

3. Which of the following is **not** an example of internal growth? Select **one** answer.
   A Mars increases market share of snacks due to increased sales of its latest product
   B Cadbury's new advertising campaign leads to 8% increase in sales of its chocolate
   C Nestle proposes a takeover of US producer Hershey
   D Thornton's new low fat chocolate bar causes a 15% increase in sales revenue

ResultsPlus — Build Better Answers

Which of the following is a method of external growth available to a business? Select **one** answer. (1)
A Reinvesting profits
B Merging with another business
C Investing in research and development
D Changing the marketing mix

Answer B

Technique guide: There is a number of choices available.

Think: What is internal and external growth and how are they different? What internal and external methods lead to growth for a business?

Then: consider the alternatives.

A is incorrect as reinvesting profits is an internal method of growth. It involves taking profits made by the business from previous years and ploughing them back so that the business increases its productive potential. ■

C is incorrect as investing in research and development is an internal method of growth. It involves the R&D department creating new products that the business can produce and sell to customers so that its sales grow. ■

D is incorrect as changing the marketing mix is an internal method of growth. It involves changing the price, promotion, product or place where a product is provided to customers in order to better meet customers' needs and increase sales. ■

B is correct. Merging is an method of external growth. It involves joining with another business that is **outside** and **separate** from the organisation. ▲

11 Why do businesses grow?

Case Study

In September 2006 Geoff and Sallyann Kilby decided to try to expand their farming business. Knowing that people were becoming more health conscious they decided to produce a high quality cooking oil from the rapeseed they grow on their farm in the Wharfe Valley, West Yorkshire. The oil is much healthier than traditional cooking oils and could be marketed as a healthy alternative.

The Kilbys have recently invested in machinery which allows the production to increase from 1,500 bottles per year to 6,000 bottles a month, for example. This has enabled the business to take advantage of economies of scale. For example, bottling used to be a job for four people, who could fill 300 bottles per hour. Investment in a new filling machine system enabled 1,000 bottles per hour to be filled, with just one operator. The filling machine cost £106,000.

The reason they wanted to grow was to take advantage of the market that existed for healthy products. In doing so this would increase their returns from their business

Their oil is now firmly established in a competitive market. It is seen regularly on TV cookery programmes and is a favourite of celebrity chef James Martin. In 2008 Wharfe Valley Farms was awarded the title 'Business of the Year' by *Business and Industry* magazine.

Source: adapted from business interview.

Objectives

- To identify at least five benefits of growth for businesses.
- To understand what is meant by market power.
- To define economies of scale and give examples.
- To understand different reasons why businesses want to grow.
- To understand the drawbacks of business growth.
- To define economies of scale.

edexcel key terms

Economies of scale – the factors which cause the average cost of producing something to fall as output rises.

Why do businesses want to grow?

Wharfe Valley Farms wanted to grow in size by developing a new product and to diversify into new markets. Ultimately, the reason for this growth was to generate more revenue and higher profits. This may seem an obvious statement, but the reasons why businesses want to grow are not as straightforward as might appear. Reasons include:

- survival - larger businesses have a greater chance of survival. Greater revenue means that money can be re-invested into the business to further improve the chances of survival;
- larger returns for owners - a larger business has greater revenue streams than a smaller business. This may lead to higher profits for the owners;
- **economies of scale** - operating on a larger scale can mean that average costs of production are reduced. This can also lead to greater profitability;
- spreading the risk - where a business grows by developing a new product, or by branching into new markets, then risk can be spread and therefore reduced.

Benefits of business growth

There are many benefits to be gained from being a large organisation. One benefit involves the idea of **economies of scale**. These are the factors which cause the average or unit cost of producing something to fall as output rises. For example, if Wharfe Valley Farms grows to produce 100,000 litres of oil a month from 50,000 litres, it has increased output by 100%. If the total cost of producing 50,000 litres was £50,000 then the average or unit cost of production would be £1 per litre. As a result of growing to produce 100,000 its total costs are likely to rise. If its total costs rise to £75,000 this would mean that its **average costs** will fall to 75p per litre. Another way of referring to economies of scale is 'the advantage of size'.

Bigger businesses have other advantages over their smaller counterparts. Some of the benefits are straightforward to recognise. Operating on a larger scale should result in higher revenue and higher profits. This will please owners who will see greater returns from their investment and can also allow the business to re-invest in improving the business.

Bulk-buying economies of scale - an individual example

Many large businesses are able to exploit their size to negotiate discount prices from suppliers or are able to buy such large quantities that they are able to reduce their average costs. These are referred to as commercial economies of scale. As individuals we can see a simple example of how this might work.

The popular cereal, Weetabix, is sold in boxes of 12, 24 and 48 which are priced at £1.22, £1.78 and £3.24 respectively. The **average cost** of each Weetabix is therefore 10p, 7.4p and 6.5p. Anyone prepared to buy the largest box of Weetabix will reduce their average costs by 35%. This is an example of **bulk-buying economies** of scale as the decision to buy on a larger scale brings down average cost.

Technical economies of scale occur when businesses use advanced machinery and technology to bring down the average cost of production. Bigger businesses can use bigger and better machinery.

Greater size and greater power

In most markets there is a combination of producers, from those on a very small scale to those who operate on a large scale. In grocery retailing, some businesses are very small scale, a single shop in many cases, whilst at the other extreme some retailers have many outlets. The major supermarkets, for example, have hundreds of stores. 70% of the UK population use Tesco at some point each year. This type of market share can give businesses enormous **market power**. This is a measure of the influence of a business over consumers and suppliers.

Market power is closely linked to market share. The higher the market share, the greater the market power is likely to be. For example, where a business is the only supplier in a market (a monopoly) it has a great deal of market power as customers do not have the option of competing products. Potentially this business could charge higher prices, safe in the knowledge that customers cannot shift their spending to a rival.

Similarly with suppliers, if a large business is the main customer of a small supplier, then it has a lot of influence over the supplier. An example is shown in Figure 1. As a major customer for many small suppliers, Boots was able to exert its market power.

Buying larger boxes of a cereal brings down the average cost

Figure 1 – Alliance Boots

In 2008 Alliance Boots, owner of the Boots the Chemist, informed all of its UK suppliers that it was extending the period in which it would pay for goods received from 30 days to 75 days. This upset many suppliers who in many cases relied on Boots as their main customer. As they did not have other customers of the same size, they had to accept the new terms. In this case Alliance Boots was exerting its market power over its suppliers.

This type of market power is good for the business with the power, but less good for customers and suppliers. For Alliance Boots the ability to pay suppliers later means that cash flow can be improved. Similarly with prices, market power allowing higher prices to be charged can be good for the bottom line - profit.

Source: adapted from www.fpb.org.

edexcel key terms

Bulk-buying (commercial) economies – occur when businesses can gain discounts on large orders from suppliers.

Technical economies of scale – reductions in average costs of production due to the use of more advanced machinery.

Market power – a measure of the influence of a business over consumers and suppliers.

11 Why do businesses grow?

Are there any drawbacks to business growth?

It might appear that business growth is always a good thing. It will lead to greater returns for the business and should lead to lower average costs of production as economies of scale exist. Growth may lead to increased market power, which will give the business greater influence over suppliers and customers. However, this is simplifying the matter. Growth is not always good. It can sometimes have some unintended consequences.

Big businesses can make the wrong decisions. ITV is a media company and is responsible for many popular TV programmes, such as Coronation Street. In 2005 it purchased Friends Reunited, a social networking website, for £175 million. ITV wanted to expand into what it considered to be growth areas. However, the decision proved to be costly. At this time other social networking websites were taking off. Facebook and Bebo were both popular with younger audiences and quickly became more popular than Friends Reunited. Figures show Facebook users rose from 2.7 million to 13.4 million from March 2007 to March 2008, while Bebo rose from 7.8m to 11.6m. Over the same period Friends Reunited saw user numbers drop from 4.3 million to 2.4 million. By 2009 ITV wanted to sell Friends Reunited - and for less than half of what it originally paid. The decision to buy Friends Reunited proved to be costly for ITV.

This example illustrates the difficulties which can arise when businesses achieve growth. In seeking to expand and become even bigger, ITV found that it had made a wrong decision. Because of the scale of their organisation, big businesses can lose focus and make poor decisions.

Diseconomies of scale

Diseconomies of scale are the factors which cause average costs of production to increase as output increases. In other words, as a business becomes bigger, its costs of producing each unit of output rise. This can be for a number of reasons. Co-ordination of the business may become more difficult. Making sure individuals and teams are doing what they should be doing becomes less straightforward when a business is very large. Communication within the business can become more problematic.

For Vision, in Figure 2, communication and co-ordination are not an issue. Hattie can communicate directly with her employees and make sure that information is passed on directly. In very large businesses, communication and decision-making is much more challenging. In very large firms, some workers may feel that they are not really part of the organisation, that they are a small cog in a very large wheel and become alienated as a result. This can reduce their productivity. Large firms may also lose their ability to adapt quickly to changes in the market and this can lead to them losing out to competition.

Globalisation has increased the possibility of communication and co-ordination difficulties. With businesses increasingly working with a range of suppliers and contractors, often in different countries, the chance of diseconomies of scale arising are increased. A clothing retailer in the UK which has ordered a specific type of product from a supplier in China is a long way from the supplier to answer any queries or address any problems.

In 2008 Primark axed its contacts with three suppliers in India after it discovered they were using child labour. The fact that Primark was located thousands of miles away was one reason why it could not keep a close control over its suppliers.

However, the developments in ICT are helping to overcome these difficulties. The Internet and email, and associated technologies, mean that businesses can communicate much more effectively than ever before. Web-conferencing and webcasting take this a stage further, and mean that the likelihood of poor communication is being reduced. In other words, ICT is helping to reduce the disadvantages associated with the growth of businesses.

Source: adapted from http://www.guardian.co.uk/media/2008/apr/29/itv.digitalmedia, www.telegraph.co.uk.

Figure 2 – Small businesses can avoid diseconomies of scale

Hattie Phillips is a sole trader who owns a hair salon - Vision. She employs one full-time stylist, Talisa, and one part-time assistant, Holly. As the business is in one location, Hattie feels that she can monitor the work of her two employees closely. If the salon has few customers, Harriet will ensure that time will be spent cleaning equipment or practising new styles. She ensures that both Talisa and Holly are focussed and make full use of their time. In this way the business operates efficiently. This is relatively easy to do as the business is so small.

edexcel key terms

Diseconomies of scale – the factors which cause average costs of production to increase as output increases.

Over to you

In February 2009 Royal Bank of Scotland (RBS) announced the worst loss in UK corporate history. During the financial year 2008-9 RBS made a loss of £24 billion. The chairman of RBS was forced to leave his job. In addition to the loss RBS faced the further difficulty that many of its loans were not likely to be re-paid. The bank had been reckless in its lending and now faced the prospect of bankruptcy. This led the government to step in to safeguard the bank and people's money.

This disastrous episode came after RBS had been actively seeking to grow. In 2007 RBS carried out a takeover of the Dutch bank ABN Amro, which it bought for 17 billion. By 2008 it was clear that ABN Amro was not worth the money RBS had paid. Lots of ABN Amro's assets were worthless.

RBS, in seeking to grow, had taken over a business which was not worth the money. The strategy of growth had backfired.

Source: adapted from newspaper articles, various.

1. Identify **two** reasons why RBS might have wanted to take over ABN Amro. (2)
2. Explain **one** advantage for a business such as RBS of growing in size. (3)
3. Explain **one** disadvantage for a business such as RBS of growing in size. (3)

Test yourself

1. Which of the following is the **best** definition of economies of scale? Select **one** answer.

   A *Factors which cause a reduction in total costs as output increases*
   B *Factors which cause an increase in total costs as output increases*
   C *Factors which cause average costs to fall as output increases*
   D *Factors which cause average costs to rise as output increases*

2. Which of the following is **not** a benefit which occurs when a business grows in size? Select **one** answer.

   A *Increased sales revenue*
   B *Higher profit*
   C *Higher average costs*
   D *Greater returns for owners*

3. Egglestone Catering was formed in 1999 by Josh Egglestone and his brother Adam. The original business was one mobile catering unit which worked at local events and functions, as well as on matchdays in Sheffield. Since 2001 the business has grown rapidly and now has 31 catering units which can be hired for functions. The business now has 15 full time employees plus another 30 temporary staff. Josh has found that keeping track of costs has become difficult as the business has grown is size. Which of the following **best** explains the problem he is experiencing? Select **one** answer.

   A *Increased market power*
   B *Diseconomies of scale*
   C *Economies of scale*
   D *Market share*

ResultsPlus
Build Better Answers

(i) What is meant by the term diseconomies of scale? (1)

(ii) Explain **one** method that a large firm might use to try and reduce the effect of diseconomies of scale in the organization. (3)

Think: What are diseconomies of scale? How do they affect a business? What strategies might a business use to reduce them?

■ **Basic** A definition of diseconomies of scale, such as the rise in average costs arising from increased scale of production. (1)

● **Good** A definition of diseconomies of scale and an identification of a method with some explanation of how it might prevent diseconomies. For example, 'Improving communication could help reduce the costs of sending messages in a large business.' (2)

▲ **Excellent** A definition of diseconomies of scale and an identification of a method with a clear explanation of how it might prevent diseconomies. For example, 'Improving communication could prevent diseconomies of scale in a large organisation. As businesses grow, communication becomes more involved and costly. There may be costs associated with delays, incorrect messages being sent and received or costly communication systems Ensuring good communication, perhaps with an effective e-mail or intranet, could improve efficiency and reduce average costs of communication.' (4)

12 Monopoly power - good or bad?

Case Study

Wrigley controls 95% of the market for chewing gum in the UK, with brands such as Extra, Orbit, Airwaves and Hubba Bubba. It has held a long time monopoly in the market which has sales worth £400 million per year. The market for chewing gum had for some time been seen as one lacking innovation or variety.

In 2007 Cadbury Schweppes launched a new product in a bid to challenge the dominance of the Wrigley brands. Trident, the new chewing gum from Cadbury-Schweppes, was launched with a huge television advertising campaign. Trident was designed as a more exciting chewing gum, with different packaging and flavours such as Apricot and Tropical Twist. It was the intention of Cadbury-Schweppes to encourage people to chew gum for fun, not just for fresher breath.

Wrigley responded to its new competitor with its own new products, such as Extra Fusion, its own liquid-filled product with flavours such as orange mango.

Source: adapted from www.brandrepublic.com.

Objectives

- To define monopoly and give examples.
- To understand how businesses can build monopoly power.
- To understand the negative effects of monopoly on different stakeholder groups.
- To understand that monopolies can have some benefits for society.

edexcel key terms

Monopoly – a business which has a market share of 25% and can therefore influence the market. In a pure sense a monopoly exists when there is only one seller.

What is monopoly?

In a pure sense **monopoly** means 'one seller'. In reality pure monopolies are rare, although there are some good examples. Water is one such example. If you were to move house to Derbyshire and decided you wanted a water supply, you have one option: Severn Trent Water. There is only one supplier of water in this region of the UK. However, a business can be said to be a monopoly when it has some degree of **market power**, even if it not the only seller in a market.

Market power involves a business having the ability to exert some control over the market, for example by charging higher prices than would exist if there was competition. In theory Severn Trent Water could charge whatever price it wished to consumers in its area. Customers would not have the option to choose another supplier. The business would have total market power. Of course, if it charged too high a price some people may not be able to afford to have water. One of the problems of monopolies, however, is that they may charge higher prices than if there was competition in the industry. In fact, the government regulates the actions of some monopolies, in terms of the prices they can charge. This will be covered in the next section.

The Government defines a business as having monopoly power if it has a 25% market share and above. The Government regards this level of market share as providing too much market power.

In the case study above, Wrigley had, and indeed still has, clear market power. Its brands dominate the market for chewing gum. This is despite the attempts by rivals, such as Cadbury-Schweppes' Trident, to try to break into the market. Wrigley has a monopoly in the market for chewing gum. But does this matter? In a word, yes. It matters to the whole range of stakeholder groups connected with the market. For consumers they potentially have to buy a product which may be more expensive than would be the case if competition existed. For consumers the existence of monopoly power can bring disadvantages. For the shareholders of Wrigley the monopoly is a good thing. The market power of their products means that sales and profits are likely to be higher than would be the case if lots of chewing gum manufacturers were competing with one another.

In evaluating the effects of monopoly it is important to consider different stakeholder viewpoints.

Monopoly - bad?

The disadvantages of monopoly are easy to identify. These focus on the impact upon consumers and competitors. Monopoly gives a business the opportunity to charge higher prices and at the same time restrict the ability to rivals to enter the market. Wrigley spends huge sums on advertising to ensure its brands remain popular. Such spending is seen as a barrier to entry - a means of trying to prevent other firms from being able to enter the market easily to develop competition. A new business entering the market will struggle to establish the same identity and recognition for their product. There are certain disadvantages of monopoly power.

Price Where little competition exists businesses can charge higher prices, safe in the knowledge that this price cannot be 'competed down'.

Choice Another criticism of monopoly is that it restricts choice for consumers. Henry Ford, the founder of the Ford Motor Company, in 1908 launched a new motor car which would soon dominate the market. The Model T was a sensation, and by 1918, half of all cars in America were Model Ts.

Ford is famous for his statement that, 'Any customer can have a car painted any colour that he wants - so long as it is black'. The example here is that if, early in the last century, you wanted a car, you had very little choice. If you wanted a Ford car, you had no choice of colour.

We don't need to go back a hundred years to identify examples of monopoly restricting choice. This can happen on a local level, as well as on a national and international level. In some rural communities local shops, petrol stations and public houses have **local monopolies**. If a community has just one petrol station, with the nearest alternative many miles away, then the local business has a monopoly. Local people have no alternatives and therefore have little choice.

On a national level the Royal Mail has a monopoly on mail delivery for non-business consumers. On a wider level, Microsoft holds significant market power due to its monopoly in the market for computer operating systems, with Windows being loaded on over 90% of all computers.

Excessive profits Monopolies can often make very high profits because of the lack of competition. Microsoft makes billions of dollars in profits. This money is paid to shareholders and ploughed back into the business, for product development and

> **ResultsPlus**
> **Watch Out!**
>
> Deciding whether a monopoly is good or bad depends on the perspective you are looking from. For a consumer monopoly may be a bad thing due to the possibility of high prices. However, shareholders are likely to be more pleased with a monopoly position as this can generate higher revenue and returns.

Royal Mail has a monopoly on certain letter deliveries

Local monopolies exist where there are few other businesses in the area

12 Monopoly power - good or bad?

other factors. Part of the explanation for these high levels of profit is made because of the lack of competition in this market.

Monopoly - good?

The case against monopoly seems to be strong. However, there are advantages to be gained from monopoly, and not just for the owners of a business lucky enough to have a monopoly position.

Value for money Large businesses can often negotiate lower prices for their raw materials and components. They can take advantage of bulk buying economies of scale. In theory at least, monopolies can produce at lower average costs than smaller businesses and can therefore charge lower prices.

Developing new products The cost of developing new products can be extremely high and can take many years. Without some form of monopoly power some product development would not take place. In the pharmaceuticals industry businesses seek **patents** to protect their ideas, giving them a legal monopoly. A patent is the legal protection for a product. It ensures that no other business can steal a business's ideas. In other words it gives the business a monopoly in the use of its own ideas. This encourages product development and innovation. When Steve Jobs, the boss of Apple, launched the iPhone in 2007, he announced, 'And boy have we patented it!'. This was as much a message to other phone companies as to the waiting world.

Natural monopolies A **natural monopoly** is where one large business can supply the market with products at lower costs than many producers could. The large business would be able to gain economies of scale. Examples might be gas or water supply. There would also be a great waste and duplication of resources if there were many producers supplying the same product. Imagine the waste if there were many businesses setting up pipes or wires all next to each other to supply services such as water, gas or electricity.

Figure 2

In 2009 GlaxoSmithKline, a large pharmaceutical maker, announced that is was to cut prices for its drugs in poor countries. The business aimed to charge a maximum of 25% of the price charged in developed countries. These drugs were for many illnesses common in third world countries. As a large business with patents on many of its products, GlaxoSmithKline had been able to develop products which were helpful for society. The cost of developing new drugs runs into millions of pounds and few small businesses can afford to do it. Large firms like GSK would not develop these life saving drugs if there was not some commercial return on their investment. They can gain this by having a monopoly on production through a patent, Its monopoly of certain products meant that it was able to offer products at lower prices. This is also an example of a business demonstrating its ethical responsibility.

Source: adapted from Wall Street Journal, 14.2.2009.

---

edexcel key terms

Patent – a legal protection for a business's new ideas. This prevents other businesses stealing ideas from other companies.

Natural monopoly – where one large business can supply the market with products at lower costs than if the market was supplied by many producers.

Test yourself

1. Which of the following is the **best** definition of monopoly? Select **one** answer.

   A A business which has the largest market share in an industry
   B Where a business which has a market share of 25% or more and can therefore influence the market
   C Where many businesses compete in a market, providing consumers with lots of choice
   D Where a business is owned by one person, such a sole trader

2. Mark Sorsby owns a general store in a small village in the Lake District. The store sells a wide range of goods, from food to firewood, and is very important to local people. The nearest shop is 14 miles away. Mark's business is a local monopoly. Which of the following is **most likely** to be an **advantage** to Mark of having this monopoly power? Select **one** answer.

   A A good reputation with local customers
   B The ability to charge higher prices
   C A good brand image
   D Greater power over suppliers

3. Monopolies are often large businesses and have a large degree of market power. This can be bad for consumers, but can have some advantages. Which of the following is **not** an example of a disadvantage of a business having monopoly power? Select **one** answer.

   A The ability to develop new products
   B High prices
   C Less choice for consumers
   D Excessively high profits

12 Monopoly power - good or bad?

Over to you

Toyota is the world's largest car-maker, employing over 300,000 people around the world. As an established car-maker with a recognised brand name, Toyota has a degree of market power. This enables the business to make huge profits. For example, in 2007 Toyota's profit was over 2,200 billion yen - equivalent to over £15 billion.

In 2008 Toyota announced that it had sold its 1 millionth Prius, the petrol-electric hybrid car much celebrated by environmentalists. The car was launched in 2001, although it had been on sale in Japan since 1997. The Prius was the first mass-produced hybrid car and has one of the lowest emissions of carbon dioxide and other greenhouse gases. This makes the Prius an important development trying to address what cars create in relation to global warming.

The development of the Prius cost Toyota hundreds of millions in terms of the new technology. By using its profits for this type of development, the environment should benefit due to transport with fewer emissions of carbon dioxide.

Source: adapted from: http://www.toyota.co.jp/en/ir/financial_results/2007/year_end/summary.pdf

1. What is meant by market power? (2)

2. Explain **one** disadvantage for a consumer of a business becoming too big. (3)

3. Using the evidence above, and your knowledge of business and economics, assess the extent to which a large business such as Toyota might have a negative impact on different stakeholder groups. (10)

ResultsPlus
Build Better Answers

Explain how a monopoly might **benefit** customers. (3)

Think: What is a monopoly? Why do monopolies exist? What type of businesses might be monopolies? How might the activities of monopolies differ from businesses in competitive markets?

🟥 **Basic** A simple reason given. For example 'a monopoly might be able to develop new products for consumers.' (1)

🟠 **Good** Explanation of why a monopoly might benefit consumers. For example 'New products for customers are expensive to develop. Monopolies can afford to do this, knowing they can make large profits from their monopoly position.' (2)

🔺 **Excellent** Clearly explains why a monopoly might benefit consumers. For example 'The cost of developing new products can be high and take years. Monopolies may be prepared to accept the cost of R&D, knowing they can make profits, as they have little competition. Customers may benefit from a choice of products that may not, otherwise, have been developed.' (3)

13 Can big business be controlled?

Case Study

BAA is an airport operator which owns seven airports in the UK, including Heathrow Airport. In 2009 the Competition Commission, the government body responsible for ensuring that competition is encouraged in different markets, signalled that BAA would need to sell off three of its airports - Gatwick, Stansted and Edinburgh or Glasgow. The Competition Commission decided that a forced sell off was the best way to introduce competition into airports in the Soth East of England, and in Scotland. In explaining the decision, the chairman of the Commission, Christopher Clarke, stated that: 'Under the ownership of BAA, there is no competition. Under separate ownership, the airport operators, including BAA, will have a much greater incentive to be far more responsive to their customers, both airlines and passengers'. In other words, the Competition Commission believed that BAA had too much market power and that consumers were getting a bad deal as a result.

Source: adapted from
http://www.independent.co.uk/news/business/news/watchdog-set-to-force-airports-selloff-1193271.html, http://comments.theherald.co.uk

Objectives

- To know the role of the Competition Commission and other competition authorities.
- To understand reasons why the competition authorities investigate acquisitions of businesses.
- To know what is meant by self regulation and give examples.
- To evaluate the effectiveness of self regulation in the UK.
- To define pressure groups and give examples.
- To understand the role of pressure groups in influencing the behaviour of business.

edexcel ::: key terms

Regulators – independent bodies set up by the Government to monitor and regulate business activity.

What is the role of the Government?

The above example illustrates how important the government believes competition in any industry is. The Competition Commission is a body set up by the Government to investigate issues of competition to ensure that the public interest in maintained. In the case of BAA above, the concern was that BAA owns two of the three main airports in London, Gatwick and Heathrow. In so doing there is a concern that BAA might be in a position where it can exploit its monopoly power and charge airlines and retail outlets that are located in the airports too high a price and offer a service that is not as good as would be the case if there was more competition.

The **Competition Commission** was created by the Competition Act of 1998 and was given wider powers by the Enterprise Act 2002. It investigates mergers, markets and regulated industries under UK competition law. It cannot investigate itself, but considers complaints by the public or cases referred to it by bodies such as the Office of Fair Trading (OFT). It can make decisions and can take action to where an inquiry has identified problems. These include blocking mergers, forcing companies to sell off assets and making changes to the way markets operate. Any business with a market share of greater than 25% is subject to investigation by the Competition Commission.

Regulation: controlling big business

Regulators are independent bodies set up by the Government to monitor and regulate business activity. The Competition Commission is one of the main regulators of UK business.

Separate regulators exist for the former nationalised industries like gas, electricity, water, the railways and the telephones. These industries were previously state monopolies and as such competition was limited or even non-existent.

Figure 1 – Ofwat ready to break up water monopolies

The regulator of the water industry, Ofwat, has announced that competition is to be introduced into the market. This is to break up the monopolies which currently exist in specific areas. The focus will initially be for business customers, such as industrial plants and hospitals. This has already been done in Scotland, where 100,000 business customers can choose their own water supplier. Ofwat believes that the break up of the local monopolies will introduce greater price competition into the market, which will be better for customers.

Source: adapted from http://business.timesonline.co.uk/tol/business/industry_sectors/utilities/article3945519.ece

When they were **privatised** the Government introduced a system of regulators to ensure these industries did not abuse their market power and operated in the public interest.

A regulator was appointed for each industry that has the power to set the prices and enforce decisions which make the industry more competitive. The water industry is regulated by The Office of the Water Regulator (Ofwat). Gas and electricity are regulated by The Office of the Gas and Electricity Markets (Ofgem). Other regulators are:
- The Office of Rail Regulation (ORR) which regulates the rail industry;
- The Office of Communications (OFCOM) which regulates the communications industry.

Where competition exists there is no need for this type of direct regulation. The existence of competition acts to control the actions of businesses. In this sense the market itself is the 'regulator'. For example, assume a new pizza takeaway opens in an area where five other takeaways already exist. The new business decides to charge a price which is double that of its competitors. What would happen next? The business is not breaking the law. It can charge what price it wants. No government body will intervene to insist that it charges a lower price: currently no regulator exists in the market for takeaway pizza simply because consumers have plenty of choice. However, the market will influence the decisions of the business. By charging a price much higher than competitors the business may lose customers to its rivals unless its pizzas are in some way of such high quality that they justify the price being charged. The existence of a large number of choices means that each business has to justify its existence either through the price it charges or the quality of the product and the service that it provides.

With the large utilities like water, gas and electricity, the choice may not be present and so industry regulators effectively operate to make their industries behave as if competition did exist. The regulators' areas of responsibility are:
- prices - the regulator monitors and can set the prices that the industries can charge;

edexcel key terms

Privatisation – the transfer of state owned businesses to the private sector.

13 Can big business be controlled?

> **Figure 2** – The EU Competition Commission
>
> In 2007 The EU Competiton Commission ruled that 'interchange fees' charged by MasterCard on 'cross-border transactions' within the EU broke the EU rules on restrictive trade practices. Interchange fees are a charge on each payment at a retailer when the payment is processed.
>
> The Commission ruled that this charge inflated the cost of acceptance by retailers. Competition Commissioner Neelie Kroes said 'Consumers foot the bill, as they risk paying twice for payment cards, once through annual fees to their bank and a second time through inflated retail prices paid not only by card users but also by customers paying cash.' MasterCard had six months to comply.
>
> In 2008 MasterCard removed the charge, but appealed against the decision.
>
> Source: adapted from www.euractiv.com, www.glgroup.com

- monitoring the quality of service provided;
- seeing that the business is acting in the **public interest**.

EU regulation

The UK is a member of the European Union. Businesses in the UK are affected by European Union laws or directives, as well as UK law. They are also controlled by EU bodies, such as the EU Competition Commission. This has a similar role to the UK's Competition Commission in the UK, but in all European countries. An example of its activities is shown in Figure 2.

Is self-regulation a better option?

Competition authorities, such as the Competition Commission, and industry regulators like Ofwat, as well as Europe-wide regulation, exist to control business activity. There is another example of regulation which can exist - **self-regulation**. This is where an industry monitors its own

> **Figure 3** – The Portman Group
>
> The Portman Group is an organisation made up of representatives of the largest UK alcohol producers. The Portman Group was established to regulate the actions of this industry. Among its aims are to encourage drinks producers to promote their products responsibly, and ensure that packaging and products do not promote excessive drinking, especially among young people. The group also established the 'drinkaware' website, which is 'the main source of sensible drinking advice for consumers'. By seeking to effectively self-regulate, The Portman Group aims to demonstrate to the government and to competition authorities that additional regulation is not needed. Other industries which have self regulation guidelines in the UK include the media and toy producers.
>
> Source: adapted from portmangroup.org.uk.

actions to ensure that its businesses operate in the public interest.

Firms in the industry agree to subscribe to a code of conduct that they will be bound by. There may be a body set up by the industry to help pull together and monitor what goes on in that industry. For example:

- The Financial Services Authority (FSA) which regulates the financial services industry which includes banks, insurance and pension companies and so on;
- The Portman Group which regulates the alcoholic drinks industry, as explained in Figure 3;
- The Independent Press Complaints Commission (IPCC) which monitors the newspaper industry.

Critics argue that industry cannot regulate itself because it has too much self interest. Its supporters say that self-regulation can work and in any case the fear is that ultimately the Government could impose an independent regulator if it was not doing its job properly. However, the fact that self-regulation exists does not mean that other competition rules do not apply to these industries. So, the Competition Commission would intervene if, for example, a merger in the media industry led to a business gaining a market share of more than 25%.

Pressure groups

The idea that regulation will always produce outcomes which are desirable for all stakeholder groups is mistaken. Sometimes businesses do not act in a way that is viewed as ethical. Where regulation does not work, and where

edexcel key terms

Self-regulation – where an industry body made up of representatives from businesses within the industry monitors the actions of members to ensure rules and guidelines are followed.

businesses continue to act in a way that some stakeholder groups find objectionable, then this can lead to action by pressure groups and other organisations.

A **pressure group** is an organisation which aims to influence the decisions of businesses, government and individuals. There are hundreds of pressure groups in the UK, campaigning on matters from environmental protection to human rights. For example, Friends of the Earth operates on environmental matters, whereas Surfers Against Sewage campaigns for clean, safe recreational waters around the coast of the UK. Almost 8 million people in the UK belong to trade unions, which represent the interests of workers and negotiate with businesses on their workers' behalf.

Pressure groups can be a big influence on the actions of business. The supermarket Tesco has faced lots of action from a range of pressure groups. One such group, Tescopoly, organises to prevent the continued growth of the supermarket. Tescopoly argues that Tesco is damaging for consumers, suppliers, workers and communities.

Pressure groups try to bring people together so that they can have more influence than they would have had if they had acted alone. Where one person may be powerless, a group can have some influence. Through pressure groups all stakeholders can be represented and have a collective voice.

Pressure groups can be important in influencing the decisions of businesses, government and individuals. They can publicise information which makes consumers change their choices. For example, pressure group Action and Information on Sugar (AIS) campaigned against apparently 'sugar free' products which actually contained large amounts of sugar. As consumers became aware of this and chose different products, so companaies like Ribena needed to respond. The pressure group caused the businesses to change their products.

The extent to how successful pressure groups will be depends on a number of factors. One factor is the role of the Government. Many environmental pressure groups object to the expansion of Heathrow's third runway. However, the Government does not believe the project is wrong and has given it the go-ahead.

Pressure groups will use a variety of tactics to help get their message across. These might include encouraging boycotts, protests, marches, advertising campaigns, issuing leaflets and direct action which can be illegal. For example, some animal rights groups have caused damage to the houses and cars of those involved in the cosmetics testing industry and have broken into laboratories to release animals. One group even went as far as digging up and stealing the body of a relative of a family that owned a hamster farm in Staffordshire.

Figure 4 – Plane stupid

Plane Stupid is a pressure group which campaigns against the expansion of airports and air travel. It has staged demonstrations at Heathrow Airport as a protest against the expansion of this airport.

Source: adapted from www.planestupid.com.

ResultsPlus Watch Out!

Self-regulation does not mean that other forms of regulation do not apply. They do.

edexcel key terms

Pressure group – an organisation which aims to influence the decisions of businesses, government and individuals.

13 Can big business be controlled?

Test yourself

1. Which of the following situations is **most likely** to lead to action from the Competition Commission? Select **one** answer.

   A A business breaks the law by selling food which is out of date
   B Electricity suppliers increase prices by above the rate of inflation
   C The closure of a major business due to a lack of demand
   D A merger between two major businesses leads to a combined market share of 40%

2. The drinks industry is controlled by a system of self-regulation. Which of the following statements **best** explains what is meant by self regulation? Select **one** answer.

   A Where a business is run by its own workers
   B Where industry regulators, such as Ofgem, control the actions of businesses
   C A body which monitors the actions of its own businesses
   D Government intervention to prevent businesses gaining monopoly power

3. Greenpeace is a pressure group which campaigns on a range of issues connected to environmental protection. Which of the following is the **best** definition of pressure group? Select **one** answer.

   A Business groups which put pressure on consumers to buy particular goods or services
   B Employers' organisations which seek to put pressure on government to reduce taxes on business
   C An organisation which aims to influence the decisions of government
   D An organisation which aims to influence the decisions of businesses, government and individuals

ResultsPlus
Build Better Answers

Describe the role of the Competition Commission in controlling business with monopoly power. (4)

Think: What is the Competition Commission? What powers does it have? What role does it play?

■ **Basic** A simple statement is given such as 'The Competition Commission can force monopolies to stop fixing prices.' (1)

● **Good** A description is given of the activities of the Competition Commission. For example 'The Competition Commission investigates businesses that are carrying out anti-competitive practices, such as price fixing. It has the power to stop these activities.' (2)

▲ **Excellent** A clear outline of the role of the Competition Commission and how it prevents the abuse of monopoly power is given. For example, 'The Competition Commission investigates markets where existing businesses are engaging in anti-competitive behaviour. Examples of areas where it might investigate include price fixing, where businesses artificially keep prices high, or predatory pricing, where a business sells at very low price with the intent of driving competitors out of the market. If it decides that activities are not in the public interest the Commission has the power to force businesses to cease these activities.' (4)

Over to you

Energy regulator Ofgem has insisted that gas and electricity suppliers slash their prices. The call came following a period when wholesale energy prices have fallen dramatically. Ofgem is keen that these reductions in costs for the energy companies are passed onto consumers in the form of lower prices.

Phil Bentley, the managing director of British Gas, one of the energy companies, responded: 'We are fully confident we will meet all Ofgem's requirements for transparency and fairness in our pricing'.

Energy companies have been criticised by some pressure groups for not passing on the price cuts. They claim that as limited competition exists in the energy markets, companies do not have to pass on price cuts as quickly as if competition did exist.

Source: adapted from: http://business.timesonline.co.uk/tol/business/industry_sectors/utilities/article5355193.ece

1. Using an example from the evidence explain what is meant by competition. (2)

2. Explain why it is felt that industries such as gas and electricity need to have regulators like Ofgem. (3)

3. Pressure groups can have an important influence in industries where competition is limited. Assess the role of pressure groups in influencing the decisions of businesses and consumers. (8)

examzone

Know Zone: Topic 5.3
Big or Small

In this topic you have learned about: the reasons why businesses grow and how this growth can be achieved, how business can gain advantages over smaller businesses, The benefits of business growth, he drawbacks of business growth, including diseconomies of scale, what is meant by market power and monopoly, the advantages and disadvantages of monopoly, how monopolies are controlled, and the roles of competition authorities, including the Competition Commission, self-regulation and pressure groups in influencing the actions of government, businesses and individuals.

You should know...

- [ ] The difference between internal and external growth.
- [ ] How growth can be achieved by changing the marketing mix, innovation and product development, and be able to give examples.
- [ ] That external growth involves a business joining with another business, through merger or take-over.
- [ ] The difference between backward and forward vertical integration.
- [ ] What is meant by conglomeration.
- [ ] That economies of scale refer to the fall in average costs as output rises.
- [ ] How technical economies of scale and bulk-buying economies enable a business to reduce average costs.
- [ ] Some drawbacks of business growth, including diseconomies of scale.
- [ ] That monopoly, in a pure sense, means 'one seller' but in reality monopoly power can be exercised when a business has a market share of more than 25%.
- [ ] Three disadvantages of monopoly for consumers.
- [ ] That monopolies can have some advantages for consumers and society.
- [ ] What the role of the Competition Commission involves.
- [ ] That the large, previously-nationalised UK monopolies are controlled by industry regulators.
- [ ] What is meant by self regulation.
- [ ] That a pressure group is an organisation which aims to influence the decisions of businesses, government and individuals.
- [ ] Examples of pressure groups.
- [ ] How to evaluate the effectiveness of pressure groups.

Support activity

This topic has a lot of technical content. Students must work hard to secure their own understanding of this content. One way to do this is to find real world examples of the theory.

Carry out individual research into a merger or take-over which is currently in the news. Use appropriate websites or other media sources to find some relevant information. With your research produce a one page summary showing:

- Details of the merger/take-over – which businesses are involved; when will it happen; how much will it cost, etc.
- Reasons for the merger/take-over – cost savings; collaboration; one of the businesses is struggling, etc.
- Evaluation – identify the views of different stakeholders groups about the merger.

Stretch activity

Investigate the work of the Competition Commission. Use the website - http://www.competition-commission.org.uk - and in the 'investigations' section carry out research to find out what the main reason is for most Commission investigations. Produce a table to show your results:

Businesses under investigation	Reasons for investigation	Results (if completed)
BSkyB and ITV plc	Concern over market share	Ongoing

The section on 'Current Investigations' is useful, as is the search tool for previous investigations.

ResultsPlus
Maximise your marks

Hague's Ltd is a bakery in Newark, Nottinghamshire. The business owns two sites and employs 95 workers. The business produces bread which it supplies to a number of retail chains based in the Midlands. The business has grown significantly over the past three years, due mainly to its high quality products and is now working its two bakeries at full capacity and its costs are rising. The business is concerned that it is close to a point where it cannot meet the orders of customers. The directors have taken the decision to expand, but are undecided on which strategy to adopt. The two options are:

- take over a regional rival, Rogan Bakeries, which is of similar size to Hague's Ltd, but has suffered falling demand in recent years. The owners would be agreeable to a takeover by Hague's Ltd;
- increase sales of its speciality breads by increasing promotion and by trying to gain an order from a national supermarket chain.

(a) Identify **two** reasons why Hague's Ltd might want to achieve growth. (2)

(b) Explain the difference between internal growth and external growth. (3)

(c) In your opinion, which strategy should Hague's Ltd opt for? Use the evidence in the case study and your own knowledge to justify your answer. (6)

Student answer	Examiner comment	Build a better answer
(a) To increase capacity, meet orders and make more profit. To increase sales abroad by taking over a business in France.	🟥 The question asks the student to 'identify', so brief answers are fine. In this case the student is awarded one mark for the first answer which is correct. But the second answer is incorrect as it does not relate to this business.	🔺 The question refers explicitly to Hague's Ltd, so use reference to this particular case study. For example, 'to increase capacity' addresses the concern in the case study that the business does not have enough capacity to meet orders. The second example does not relate to Hague's Ltd. You are required to try to address your answer to the particular case study of Hague's Ltd, such as achieving economies of scale to reduce costs.
(b) Internal growth is where a business grows by itself, but external growth is where the business grows with another business.	🟠 The student has some idea here, but does not fully understand what either term means. The question asks you to 'explain the difference', so some development of the comparison is needed. The student does not attempt to explain the difference at all, and therefore does not access the full marks.	🔺 The question requires students to demonstrate clear understanding of both terms, so providing a definition of each is a good start. For example, 'Internal growth occurs when a business grows by increasing its own sales, for example by increased promotion. External growth is different in that it involves growing by joining with another business, for example through a merger or a takeover.'
(c) Hague's should choose the option of external growth. By taking over Rogan Bakeries the business instantly increase its capacity and will be able to meet its orders. This is its biggest problem. There is little point increasing the promotion of its existing products at the present time as it does not have the ability to meet these orders. The business needs to increase capacity in the short term. Marketing should take place when this capacity is in place.	🟠 A good response. The student makes a judgement in the first line, and then goes on to support this with evidence and with effective use of appropriate business and economics concepts. The answer is clearly applied to the case study and the student has recognised the key underlying issue with this case study – that the business does not have sufficient capacity. The student also identifies short-term versus long-term considerations, which is relevant.	🔺 The answer is strong with no glaring errors. For questions that ask you to 'assess' it is sometimes worthwhile organising into paragraphs to emphasise the opposing arguments. In this case the arguments for/against internal growth could have been dealt with in a separate paragraph.

Practice Exam Questions

Protestors in Derbyshire are celebrating success after plans by a stone business to begin quarrying near a Peak District landmark were abandoned by the business. The quarry was to be dug near to Stanton Lees, where a Bronze Age stone circle was under threat.

The business which proposed the quarry, Stancliffe Stone, proposed to extract high quality sandstone from the quarry. There is high demand for such good quality stone, and the business planned to expand.

Protestors formed the pressure group Stanton Lees Action Group. This pressure group had one objective – to stop the quarrying at Stanton Lees. Fearful of the environmental impact the scheme might have, the protestors moved in - living in caravans and in tree-houses where they remained despite bids to evict them.

Local residents were delighted with the decision. They had not wanted to see the opening of a quarry which would cause such a major impact on the local environment.

Source: adapted from www.manchestereveningnews.co.uk

(a) Using an example, define pressure group. (2)

(b) One reason why businesses such as Stancliffe stone want to grow is to achieve economies of scale. Explain how economies of scale are a benefit to a business. (3)

Topic 5.4: Is growth good?

Topic overview
This topic looks at the concept of economic growth. It examines how the production of more goods and services by businesses allows the standard of living in a country to increase. Other ways of measuring living standards are also considered. As with most economic concepts, there are costs as well as benefits and the topic will also consider the costs to society as a whole of producing more goods and services. Problems such as pollution, traffic congestion, the use of non-renewable resources, such as oil and coal, and the problem of waste will be considered. The concept of 'sustainability' will be investigated, as well as what role businesses and the Government have in ensuring that the benefits of economic growth outweigh the costs.

Case study
In 2009 Britain's first new power station for more than five years will open in the Plymouth suburb of Langage. Owned by Centrica plc and costing more than £400 million to build, it is hoped that the power station will generate enough electricity to supply up to 1 million homes. When it opens, Langage Power Station will become one of the country's cleanest and most environmentally friendly power plants since it uses gas, the cleanest fossil fuel, to produce electricity. In order to build the power station a new £90 million high-pressure gas pipeline has been constructed across Devon to feed the power station's demand for gas. Supporters of the scheme point out that the new power station will boost the region's economic activity and gross domestic product (GDP). By connecting Plymouth to the high-pressure gas network, it is hoped that this will encourage businesses that use gas in their production process to relocate to West Devon. As a result, the investment in gas infrastructure will bring jobs and a higher standard of living to a part of the country where the average income of £20,027 is more than 10% below the national average.

However, opponents of the scheme question whether a power station should be built so close to local housing, with many home owners worried about pollution, noise and the effect the power station will have on the value of their properties. Residents have already experienced congested roads, as a steady stream of construction vehicles head towards the power station site. One resident in the neighbouring suburb of Chaddlewood said 'My house will be virtually unsellable. I used to have views of open fields, soon all I will be able to see is pylons and a smoking chimney 24 hours a day'.

Environmental groups have also voiced concerns, over what they view as short-term thinking by Centrica, one of Britain's largest energy companies. As one spokesperson pointed out 'Gas is a non-renewable resource. As it runs out its price will rise making the electricity produced at Langage much more expensive'. Instead, campaigners are pushing for a greater percentage of the country's electricity to be produced using renewable sources such as wind or solar power. This is because they reduce many of the externalities associated with burning fossil fuels. One campaigner said 'instead of building carbon producing monsters we should be trying to reduce our energy usage and produce more of our electricity using sustainable sources. There is no such thing as an environmentally friendly power station that burns fossil fuels'.

The Government also wants to encourage greater use of renewable energy and has committed the UK to a target of producing 20% of its energy from renewable sources by 2020. This will involve a strategy of taxes, subsidies and new laws designed to discourage the use of fossil fuels and encourage the use of new sustainable ways of generating electricity. These involve burning rubbish to create electricity rather than using landfill and encouraging the use of biofuels instead of petrol in cars and lorries. Businesses are also being encouraged to think more carefully about their energy use and to find ways of developing new products that are more energy efficient.

Source: adapted from thisisplymouth.co.uk.

1. Why might the construction of the new power station lead to increased average incomes in West Devon?
2. Why might the residents of Chaddlewood have not welcomed the construction of the power station?
3. What is meant by the phrase 'externalities associated with burning fossil fuels'?
4. How might the Government encourage the use of more renewable ways of generating electricity?

5.4 Is growth good?

What will I learn?

What is growth? What is meant by economic growth? Why do small changes in economic growth actually amount to output measured in billions of pounds? How can we improve our economic growth rate? Should the Government spend more money on education or should we encourage firms to buy more machinery?

Does growth increase the standard of living? What is the standard of living? Can living standards be measured purely in terms of the amount of goods and services we can purchase with our income? What other ways are there of measuring living standards?

Can growth be bad? What are negative externalities? What are the costs of economic growth? What effects do negative externalities have on society and on future generations?

Can growth be sustainable? What is meant by the term 'sustainable growth'? Can the economy grow in a sustainable way? What role do renewable resources play in allowing sustainable growth to occur? How can businesses become more socially responsible and take more responsibility for the effects their operations have on society?

What can governments do? How can the Government encourage sustainable economic growth? What role do taxes, subsidies and laws play in helping to protect the environment? What effect will these policies have on businesses?

How will I be assessed?

Unit 5 is assessed by a 1 hour 30 minute written examination consisting of three sections. Section A contains multiple choice and short answer questions designed to test your knowledge and understanding of the specification. Sections B and C use pieces of evidence and will include short answer questions together with some extended writing questions. The extended writing questions are designed to focus on the higher order skills of analysis and evaluation.

14 What is growth?

Case Study

In 2003 China was the sixth largest economy in the world. By 2007 it had become larger than the United Kingdom and became the world's fourth largest economy. By 2025 it is forecasted to become the second largest and should finally topple the United States and become the largest global economy by 2050. China is rapidly becoming an economic super power and in the 4 years to 2008 it posted economic growth rates higher than 10%. In contrast the United Kingdom economy grew by between 1 and 3% per year during the same time period. This is because China is now starting to take advantage of the large amount of resources it has, namely its population of 1.4 billion people.

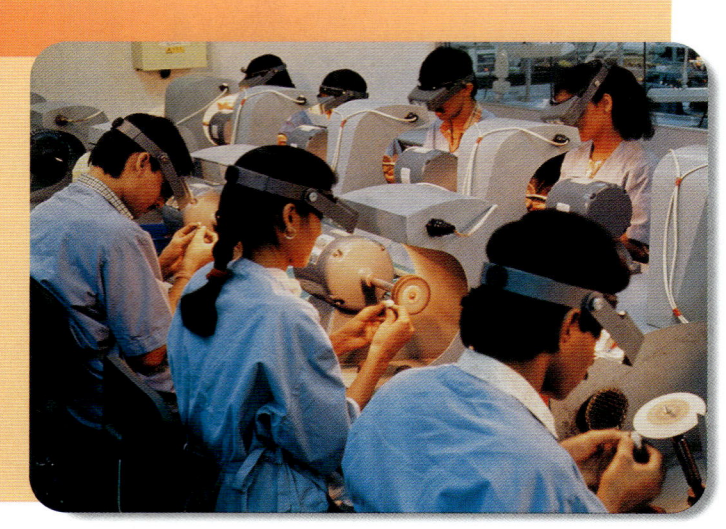

Objectives

- To understand that an economy's size is measured by the value of goods and services it produces in a year.
- To understand that economic growth rates measure how fast an economy is growing or shrinking.
- To explain how economic growth occurs.
- To appreciate the role the government plays in encouraging economic growth.

edexcel key terms

Gross domestic product (GDP) – the total value of output produced in an economy in a year.

How is the size of an economy measured?

Economic activity is about the amount of buying and selling that goes on in a country over a particular time period. Businesses produce goods and services and consumers buy them. It might be a cup of coffee and a sandwich at a café, a bike, a house, a games console, a DVD, a mobile phone, a visit to the cinema - millions of such transactions take place every day. Every second of every day goods and services are being produced by firms. For example, this book you are reading has been produced and has involved lots of resources - labour to plan and write the book, paper, printing presses, ink, advertising and promotion, editing and so on. The value of the sales of the book will form a part of the UK's annual **Gross domestic product (GDP)** figures. This is then added to all the value of all the other goods and services produced in the UK to make the total GDP figure for the year.

The size of a country's economy is measured by adding up the value of all these goods and services produced by a country in a year. Basically, a record is taken of all the goods and services produced and the price that they were sold at. This figure is called Gross Domestic Product or GDP. In an economy as large and as complicated as the United Kingdom's this is not an easy task to do. As you can imagine, the UK's GDP is extremely large and in 2007 it amounted to $2,804,437,000,000,000. This means that in 2007, $2,804 trillion worth of goods and services were produced in that year. GDP is measured in US dollars so that the size of each country's economy can be easily and more accurately compared against each other. Table 1 shows a world 'league table of GDP' for 2007.

Table 1 – League table of GDP

Rank	Country	GDP in millions of US $
1	United States	13,807,550
2	Japan	4,381,576
3	Germany	3,320,913
4	China	3,280,224
5	United Kingdom	2,804,437
155	North Korea	2,220

Source: adapted from International Monetary Fund.

What is economic growth?

Economic growth measures the change in the value of goods and services produced in an economy in a year. Assume that the only good produced in the UK was bread. In year 1, 20,000 loaves of bread were produced and each loaf sold at a price of £1. The GDP for year 1 would be £20,000. In year 2, the number of loaves of bread produced increases to 25,000. If bread prices stay at £1 then GDP is now £25,000. Expressed as a percentage change, this would give a growth RATE of 25% (5,000/20,000 x 100).

If bread production increased in year 3 to 26,000, and again, prices stayed the same, economic growth would now be 4% compared to year 2 (1,000/25,000 x 100). In this example, the rate of growth in the economy has slowed down but it is important to remember that the economy is experiencing growth. There are more loaves of bread produced in year 3 than in year 2.

If in year 4, bread production was 24,000 loaves then we can see that the number of loaves produced is actually less than in year 3 by 2,000. In this case the growth rate is negative. Economic growth would be recorded as -7.7% (-2,000/26,000 x 100). Since less has been produced in year 4 compared to year 3, we would say that the economy has 'shrunk' or 'contracted'. This is what happens when the economy is in recession - the value of goods and services produced actually falls, not just slows down.

In reality, of course, the UK produces many more goods and services than simply bread. However, the principle of calculating economic growth is exactly the same - just on a much bigger scale. Since GDP is measured in such large sums of money, economists tend to look at how an economy is progressing by looking at **economic growth** rates. This measures the percentage change in GDP in a year. Even if the percentage change is small, it can still amount to a large increase in total GDP. For instance a 0.5% increase in the UK's 2007 GDP equates to a $14,022,185,000,000 ($14 trillion) rise in the value of goods and services produced during that year. This is because 0.5% of a very large figure to start with is going to give a high total value. Equally when a country's economic growth rate is high this does not necessarily mean it has a large GDP. It just means its GDP is increasing very rapidly. For instance, if North Korea managed to achieve a 10% economic growth rate in 2007, its GDP would increase by $222,000,000,000, ($222 billion) much less than the UK's 0.5% increase in GDP. Therefore economic growth rates do not tell you the how big an economy is, they just show you how fast it is expanding or shrinking. In 2006 China's economic growth rate was 11.3%. This explains why it is moving up the table in Figure 1 so rapidly.

What causes economic growth?

Economic growth occurs when a country produces more goods and services or GDP in a year. To produce more **output** firms need to purchase more **resources**, or use existing resources more efficiently. Resources could be anything from factory buildings to machines, workers on a production line and in an office, raw materials, energy and so on. When a firm spends money on improving either the number or quality of its resources this is known as **investment**. Investment in economics refers to spending on equipment and plant that helps contribute to production.

Firms can invest money in **human capital** or **physical capital**. Investment in human capital involves improving the skills and training of workers so they can produce more output in a period of time. This happens because training a person allows them to work faster in a period of time such as an hour. When a person or machine produces more in a period of time, this is known as increasing **productivity**.

ResultsPlus Watch Out!

Productivity and production are not the same. Productivity measures how much is produced in an hour by a single person or machine. Therefore productivity measures how efficient a single person or machine is. Production on the other hand is the total amount produced by the whole firm.

edexcel key terms

Economic growth – the percentage increase in GDP per year. (This can be negative.)

Output – the amount of goods and services produced in a period of time.

Resources – the land, labour and machinery that are used to produced goods and services.

Investment – spending on equipment and plant that helps contribute to production.

Human capital investment – spending on training and education which allows workers to be able to produce more output in the future.

Physical capital investment – spending on new assets such as factories or machinery which allows a firm to produce more output in the future.

Investment in physical capital involves purchasing new assets such as a factory or a machine. A better designed factory or a brand new machine will be more productive, allowing the firm to produce more goods and services in a period of time. This increase in the firm's output will add to the country's GDP, helping to boost economic growth.

What can the Government do?

The Government also has a role in creating economic growth. It can encourage investment by firms through reducing taxes on profits. If a firm is able to keep more of the profit it makes it can use this to purchase new machinery. It can also provide grants, so that firms have access to money to either train their staff better or buy new assets. The Government can also improve the resources that it owns, allowing firms the ability to produce more. Improving infrastructure is one way in which the Government can help. Better transport links such as roads, railways and airports increase the speed with which raw materials and finished products can be delivered. It also helps people to arrive at work on time. This means firms can produce more, boosting output and GDP. Therefore a traffic jam is not just frustrating, it is actually an example of something which is holding back the UK's economic growth rate.

In less economically developed countries (LEDCs), one of the biggest obstacles to economic growth is the inability of the government to build proper roads or communication systems, provide reliable electricity supplies, have railways that help people and goods to move around the country and ports and airports to help boost trade. The government of China has spent massive amounts of money improving the infrastructure in the country. Without this investment, China would not have been able to grow as fast as it has done in recent years. However, to be able to do this, governments need money from taxes and must be able to borrow. Less economically developed countries often have problems getting the funds necessary to develop their infrastructure.

edexcel key terms

Grants – sums of money provided by the Government to encourage a particular project or activity.

Infrastructure – road, rail and air links that allow people and output to move speedily around a country and which help trade.

Less economically developed countries (LEDCs) – these are countries that have a low gross domestic product and where the average standard of living is low.

ResultsPlus Watch Out!

The word investment has many meanings. In day to day language we often refer to investing money in a bank account or investing money in shares. This is **NOT** what investment means in economics. In economics investment means spending money on assets which will increase a firm's productive capacity in the future, e.g. a new machine or extending a factory.

Test yourself

1. Gross Domestic Product (GDP) can best be defined as the total:

   A amount of goods and services produced in an economy in a year
   B amount of spending made by families in an economy in a year
   C amount of spending on physical capital made in an economy in a year
   D value of goods and services produced in an economy in a year

   Select **one** answer.

2. The country with the highest economic growth rates will have the highest:

   A level of GDP
   B level of investment
   C increase in the value of output in a year
   D infrastructure spending in a year

   Select **one** answer.

3. Firms are **most likely** to invest in human capital because:

   A demand for their product will increase
   B productivity will increase
   C it will increase the country's GDP
   D it will increase the country's economic growth

   Select **one** answer.

14 What is growth?

Over to you

The Educational Maintenance Allowance or EMA was introduced in 2004. It is designed to provide young people with an incentive to stay on at school beyond the age of 16. It does this by providing students from a family on a low income with a grant or allowance of up to £30 per week. Further bonuses of £100 are available so long as a student makes sufficient progress in their course and meet learning targets set by their school.

According to the Learning and Skills Council, EMA has been a great success. It has helped hundreds of thousands of students gain higher level courses that have helped them enter university. It has also helped cut down on the number of young people who are unemployed and has helped boost the UK's productivity. Critics of the scheme believe it is not right for taxpayer's money to be spent on paying young people to go to school. They believe that the money is better spent elsewhere on hospitals and public transport.

1. What is meant by the term 'grant'? (2)
2. Explain how EMA could improve the level of productivity in the UK. (3)
3. Identify and explain one possible drawback of the Government spending large sums of money on EMA. (3)

ResultsPlus Exam Question Report

6. Unilever is a trans-national or multi-national company operating in Indonesia. As a result of Unilever's investment, around 300,000 people earn a living based on work related to this investment. Unilever also pays taxes to the Indonesian government as a result of its work in the country.

Source: adapted from http://www.oxfam.org.uk/what_we_do/issues/livelihoods/unilever.htm

The former United Nations (UN) Secretary General, believed more multi-nationals were looking to invest in developing countries not just as a source of cheap labour but to help the countries grow and develop new skills and technologies.

Source: adapted from http://www.un.org/esa/ffd/0304-BS-Report%20on%20workshop2.pdf

Investment is an important factor in generating growth in developing countries.
(a) Define '**investment**' and explain how investment can lead to economic growth. (5) (June 2007)

How students answered

Most students (54%) scored poorly (0-1) on this question. These answers gained one mark for a simple recognition that investment involves putting money into a project with the intention of receiving a return in future, but they did not explain how investment can lead to growth.

Many students (42%) gained good marks (2-3) on this question.
These answers defined investment, for example as the purchase of capital to make other goods and services with the expectation of returns in future. They explained that investment in machinery, for example, increases the potential for more goods to be produced. This means that output of an economy increases.

Few students (4%) gained very good marks (4-5) on this question.
These answers defined investment and explained clearly how this can lead to economic growth. They took into account that investment can increase the potential for more goods and services to be produced in a number of ways. This could be investment in physical capital, such as such as machinery, factories and materials. Investment could also be in human capital, involving the education and training of workers. These would lead to an increase in future productivity and output of the economy.

15 Does growth increase the standard of living?

Case Study

In a small village in China, Weidi Zheng gets ready for another day at work. Despite China's huge economic growth and increase in Gross Domestic Product over the last ten years, Mr Zheng's standard of living has barely changed. He still lives in a house made from metal sheets, works hard in the fields for long hours and wakes in the morning to find frost and ice in his home during the cold winter months. The only benefit from China's economic miracle that he can see is that he used to burn scrap wood he collected to keep warm, now his income has risen by enough that he can afford coal. Mr Zheng is not the only person in China's 1.4 billion population to have hardly benefited from the rise in incomes and Gross Domestic Product. In 2007 196 million Chinese people lived on less than $1.25 per day.

Objectives

- To understand what is meant by the term 'standard of living'.
- To explain how improvements in GDP lead to increases in the standard of living.
- To recognise the limitations of using GDP per capita to measure the standard of living.
- To realise that measuring the quality of life can also provide further information about a country's standard of living.

edexcel key terms

Standard of living – the amount of goods and services a person can buy with their income in a year.

GDP per capita – the value of output produced by a country in a year divided by the population of that country.

What is the standard of living?

The **standard of living** refers to the amount of goods and services that a person can buy with their income. When incomes rise, a person's standard of living also rises because they can afford to purchase more goods and services. For instance, when Mr Zheng's income rose he could now afford coal rather than collecting scrap wood. In the UK the amount of goods and services that many people can afford is far higher than it was 30 years ago. UK citizens now own more cars, fridges, washing machines, dishwashers, games consoles, furniture, computers, clothes, have more insurance, go to leisure events more regularly, have their hair and nails done in salons and so on.

When a country experiences economic growth and its GDP increases, the **average** standard of living also increases for the population of that country. In the case of China, in order to increase GDP, Chinese firms had to employ more workers. As more people got jobs, incomes increased. The increased demand for labour helped to push wages up, so incomes rose further. The rise in incomes allows people to purchase more goods and services. This then meant that the average standard of living also increased.

An increase in the standard of living is often shown by looking at changes in the **GDP per capita** of a country over time. GDP per capita (or per person) measures how much output each person in the country has if the whole country's GDP were to be divided equally amongst the entire population. It is calculated by dividing GDP by the total population of a country. If a country has a population of 5 million people and its GDP for year X was $1 000 million, the GDP per capita would be $1 million/5 million = $200. This figure is often used as a measure of the average income in a country and it enables us to be able to draw comparisons between different countries and look at how standards of living have changed over time. The data in Table 1 show that during the last 10 years GDP per capita in China has increased by 289%, whilst the UK's has only risen by 83%.

The problems of using GDP

The data in Table 1 may look surprising at first glance, because it seems to suggest that the citizens of Luxembourg have the highest global living standards. However this highlights one of the main problems of relying on GDP per capita as a measure of how well off we are. If the population of a country is small, GDP per capita rates can be distorted.

Another problem is that GDP per capita assumes that all people within a country are the same. GDP per capita is an average. It assumes that everyone in a country earns the same income. Of course this is simply not the case. There will be many people who earn much less than the average income and some who earn considerably more. In some countries there are a small group of very, very rich people but many people who earn very low wages. Using GDP per capita can disguise these **income inequalities**. As a result it can have limitations in measuring the standard of living.

Table 1 suggests that the average Chinese citizen would have had an income of $3,180 per year in 2008. There will be many people enjoying incomes far higher than this and there will be many people like Mr Zheng earning far less too. The UK's GDP per capita in 2008 seems to suggest that the average person has an income of $45,681 which amounts to roughly £30,000 at the current exchange rate. A question to parents as to whether they each earn that amount highlights the limitations of using this as an accurate way of measuring the standard of living.

Can we use anything else to measure living standards?

Since there can be problems using GDP per capita, economists also use data on the **quality of life** to confirm what the GDP figures are telling them about a country's standard of living.

Infant mortality rates These are one way of showing what the quality of life is like in a country. **Infant mortality rates** measure the percentage of children who die before the age of 5. The idea is that the higher a person's standard of living, the greater the level of income they will have to spend on health care, good food, housing and clothes. These are the kind of things babies need to have a good chance of surviving past their fifth birthday. In The UK we tend not to think about infant mortality at all, since we take it for granted that almost every baby will grow into becoming an adult. However in less economically developed countries (LEDCs), this is not the case, as shown by the data in Table 2.

ResultsPlus Watch Out!

The standard of living is not the same as the quality of life. The standard of living measures how many goods and services we can buy with our income. The quality of life is how we feel about our lives and whether they are 'good' or not. The quality of life might include measures such as infant mortality rates, life expectancy etc. If a country has a high quality of life, the standard of living is usually also high - but that does not automatically mean people are happy.

edexcel key terms

Quality of life – an individual's overall sense of well being. This can be measured by health and education as well as the amount of goods and services a person can buy.

Infant mortality rates – the percentage of babies that do not survive past their fifth birthday.

Income inequalities – where there is a difference in income between different groups of people within a country.

Table 1 – How GDP per capita has changed during the last ten years

Country	1998 GDP per capita (US $)	2008 GDP per capita (US $)
Luxembourg	45,439	118,045
United States	31,689	47,025
United Kingdom	24,902	45,681
China	817	3,180
Ethiopia	129	316

Source: adapted from International Monetary Fund.

15 Does growth increase the standard of living?

Table 2 – Quality of life statistics 2008

Country	Literacy rates (%)	Infant mortality rates (%)	Life expectancy (in years)
Luxembourg	99	0.46	79.0
United States	99	0.63	78.0
United Kingdom	99	0.49	78.7
China	90.9	2.11	72.8
Ethiopia	35.9	14.5	49.2

Source: adapted from UNESCO & CIA Factbook.

Life expectancy rates Life expectancy rates are another useful measure, since again good food and high levels of health care usually lead to people living longer.

Literacy rates Other useful pieces of information include literacy rates which show the percentage of people in a country who can read and write. In a country with high living standards, parents do not need to force their children to find work, since they are not relying on their income to purchase essentials like food and clothing. This is why young people in countries like the UK have the 'luxury' of going to school. As you can see in Table 2, in Ethiopia this is not the case. Many families will not be able to afford to send their children to school and they will have to go out to find work if possible to help the family survive. If levels are low the value added by businesses in such countries tends to stay low and poverty levels persist.

In recent years, there has been much research into what makes people 'happy'. Despite earning more income and having access to more goods and services, surveys suggest people do not feel happier. Some economists believe that there are things that could be done to improve happiness which would improve the quality of life. These things include good family relationships, feelings of job security, greater control over our working lives and the balance with leisure, having friends and personal freedoms. These economists suggest that the government ought to divert investment into improving these areas of our life if our quality of life is to be really improved in the future.

edexcel key terms

Life expectancy rates – the average age which people are expected to live from birth.

Literacy rates – the percentage of adults who are able to read and write.

Test yourself

1. Infant mortality rates are a measure of:

   A the quality of living
   B the standard of living
   C GDP per capita
   D life expectancy

   Select **one** answer.

2. Look at the photographs. Which of the following best describes the order of the standard of living, starting with the highest first?

   A 2, 3, 4, 1
   B 3, 2, 1, 4
   C 2, 3, 1, 4
   D 4, 1, 3, 2

Picture 1 A woman next to her house in Africa.

Picture 2 A family home in the USA.

Picture 3 A family in an apartment in Russia.

Picture 4 A homeless person, living rough.

3. GDP per capita measures the:

   A value of output per person in a country
   B economic growth of a country per year
   C quality of life per person in a country
   D value of household spending per person

   Select **one** answer.

15 Does growth increase the standard of living?

Over to you

Figure 1 – Economic growth

Economic Growth 2008 (%)
- Nigeria: ~6.1
- Kazakhstan: ~4.4
- Thailand: ~4.5
- Ukraine: ~6.3

Figure 2 – GDP per capita

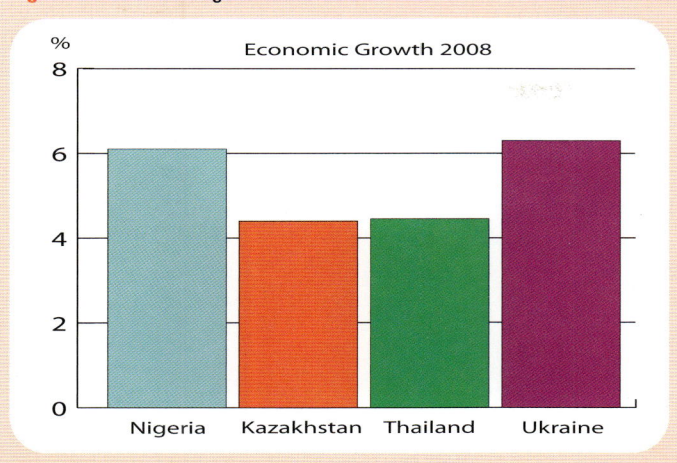

GDP per capita 2008 (US$)
- Nigeria: ~1700
- Kazakhstan: ~9000
- Thailand: ~4100
- Ukraine: ~4100

Figure 3 – Life expectancy

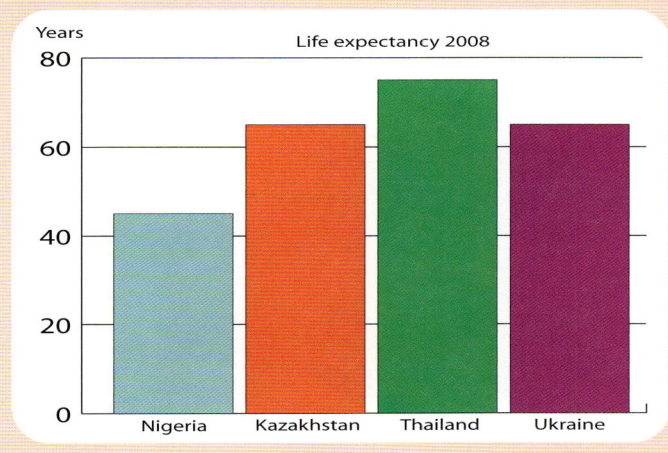

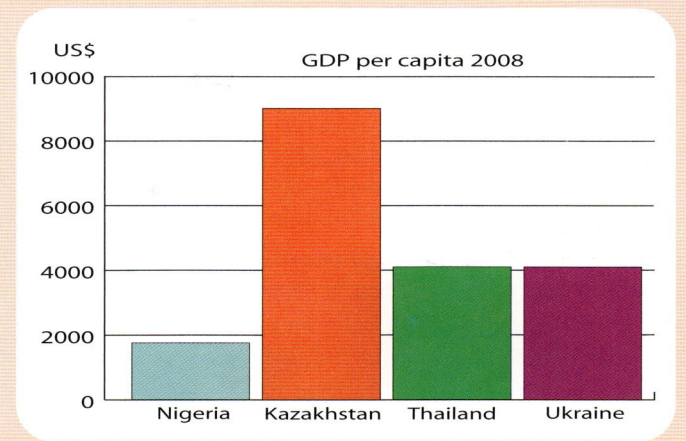

Life expectancy 2008 (Years)
- Nigeria: ~45
- Kazakhstan: ~65
- Thailand: ~75
- Ukraine: ~65

Figure 4 – GDP

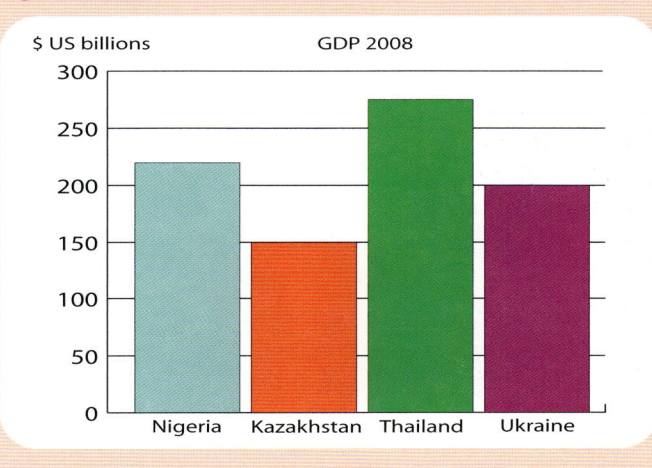

GDP 2008 ($ US billions)
- Nigeria: ~220
- Kazakhstan: ~150
- Thailand: ~275
- Ukraine: ~200

Source: adapted from International Monetary Fund.

1. Referring to the data, identify the country with the largest amount of economic activity. Explain your answer. (3)
2. Using the data, evaluate which of the four countries has the highest standard of living. (8)

ResultsPlus
Build Better Answers

Using an example, explain the meaning of the term 'standard of living'. (3)

🟥 **Basic** Provides the definition only but with no example to support it. No explanation is given. (1)

🟠 **Good** Defines the standard of living and gives an example. For example, 'The standard of living relates to the amount of goods and services people are able to buy with their income over a period of time (1), such as the number of televisions and cars people have.' (1)

🔺 **Excellent** Defines and explains the standard of living using an example. For example, 'The standard of living is the level of material comfort that people have indicated by the amount of goods and services they buy with their income in a year. (1) These could be the number of televisions, cars, DVD players or MP3 players that people have. (1) Countries with a relatively high standard of living, such as the USA, have a large proportion of the population who are able to acquire these products.' (1)

16 Can growth be bad?

Case Study

Galkino lives in the port of Aralsk, Kazakhstan. His father was a fisherman, just like his grandfather. However, Galkino will not follow in his parents' footsteps. The family's fishing boat, like those of others in the Aral Sea, is rotting on the sea bed in Aralsk harbour. Not only are there no fish, but there is also no sea. Since the 1970s the Aral Sea has been getting smaller, shrinking in size by almost two thirds. The sea once had a surface area larger than Wales, but since the 1960s its size has fallen from 68,000 Km^2 to just 17,160Km^2 in 2004. The sea has now split into three lakes, leaving the port of Aralsk at least 30kms from the edge of the water. The Aral sea disaster lays claim to being one of the world's biggest man-made environmental catastrophes, and for children like Galkino it is a clear example of how a decision to boost economic growth made in the 1950s can have devastating impacts on future generations.

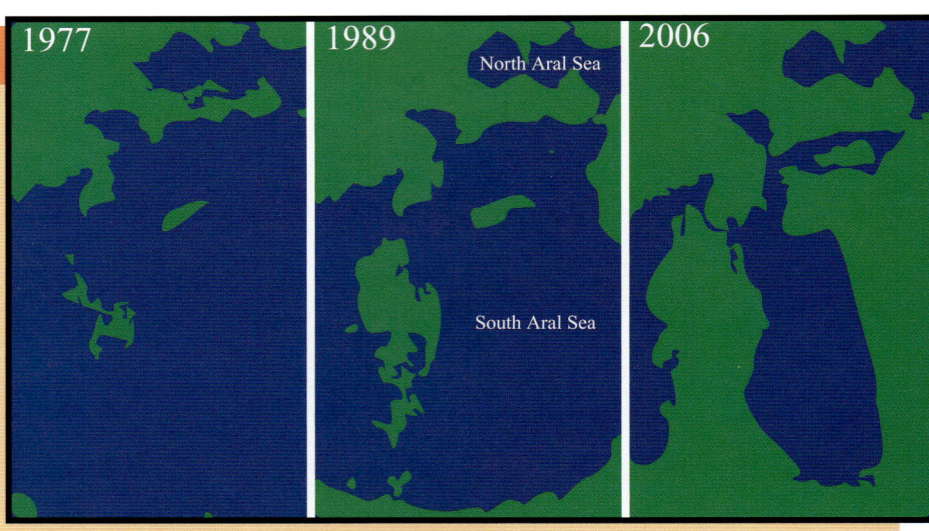

Source: adapted from http://envis.maharashtra.gov.in.

Objectives

- To understand the different types of disadvantages that are caused by economic growth.
- To understand that negative externalities are costs of a decision faced by a third party.
- To identify examples of negative externalities as a result of economic growth.
- To appreciate that negative externalities can be large and last for generations.

What are the drawbacks of growth?

It is not surprising that each country wants to boost its economic growth rate. Growth raises incomes and increases living standards for most of the population. However economic growth can have drawbacks. In the 1950s Kazakhstan was part of a much larger country called the Soviet Union, and the Soviet Government decided that the area around the Aral Sea would be an ideal place to grow cotton, thereby boosting the country's GDP. However, the decision to grow cotton in a dry desert region meant that water had to be diverted away from rivers flowing into the Aral Sea. The more water that was taken, the more the sea shrank.

To make matters worse, to increase the output of cotton, large amounts of chemical fertilisers were used. This fertiliser found its way back into the rivers and slowly over time poisoned the shrinking sea and local water supplies. This killed the fish and as the sea shrank, the climate changed. Rain fell less frequently and winters became colder, making it harder to grow crops. Average life expectancy in the area fell from 64 to 51 years. The fishing industry which used to employ 60,000 people in the 1960s has now all but vanished bringing high unemployment to former port towns such as Aralsk.

What are externalities?

The Aral Sea disaster is a striking example of how being focused on the benefits of growth can cause countries to lose sight of all the costs involved. When any decision is made, there will be costs and benefits. In many cases, some of the costs and the benefits can be estimated by those making the decision. However, those directly involved in the decision do not always think about or know what the effects will be on other people not associated with the decision. These people are called the 'third party'. A third party is affected by the decision, but had no part in making the decision in the first place.

Galkino is an example of a third party which has been affected by decisions taken over the Aral Sea. Economists call the costs and benefits of a decision on a third party **externalities**. Externalities can be **positive** and **negative**. Economic growth can create a number of important **negative externalities**.

Negative externalities

The decision to use water to grow cotton in Kazakhstan by the Soviet government may have boosted GDP in the short-term, but it also created large negative externalities to other groups of people both in the short-term and the long-term. In this case, the negative externalities were large since the decision to grow cotton destroyed the fishing industry, polluted drinking water and poisoned people. These negative externalities will be felt not just now, but for many years and generations to come.

Negative externalities are also a problem in the UK. As the UK economy has grown and more output has been produced, firms are using more and more resources like oil and coal. These **non-renewable resources** will eventually run out and using them now will force future generations to incur costs as they will have to search for alternatives.

There is a number of important externalities that occur because of economic growth.

Congestion As standards of living have improved, more people have access to cars and use them to take children to school. Parents will certainly consider the cost of the petrol and insurance and the time it takes to drive their children to school but it is unlikely that too many consider the pollution from the exhaust that adds to global warming. Many drivers complain about traffic jams without realising that they are part of the problem. Few parents may consider that in carrying out the school run they are adding to the number of cars on the road and adding to traffic congestion.

Non-renewable resources Petrol comes from a non-renewable resource, oil. One day it will run out. Parents may not consider the fact that by consuming petrol they might be preventing people in 50 years time from being able to use the same oil. These are all external costs which will have to be borne by people other than the driver of the vehicle concerned.

Waste Economic growth implies that more goods are being produced. More goods mean more packaging and more waste. This has to be disposed of. There are problems in using land fill sites to dispose of waste and alternative ways of doing so such as recycling can be expensive and use up other resources. Burning waste may also add to the problem of climate change.

Non-renewable resources will eventually run out

edexcel ⋮⋮⋮ key terms

Non-renewable resources – resources which are limited in supply and will eventually run out, e.g. oil and coal.

16 Can growth be bad?

Pollution As businesses produce more and more goods and the number of humans on the planet increases, pollution increases. This can include noise, air and water pollution. Someone, somewhere has to pay to deal with this pollution. The decision to build a new runway at Heathrow Airport will bring benefits to millions of passengers but for those living in the area around the airport the increase in noise pollution and additional congestion will be significant.

Problems like waste, congestion and pollution also create negative externalities and impose costs on people other than those who create the negative externality in the first place. There has to be a trade-off in considering the benefits of growth and the sacrifices that have to be made in order to achieve growth and an increase in living standards.

Test yourself

1. Which of the following is a non-renewable resource?

   A Petrol
   B Wind
   C Solar power
   D Fish

   Select **one** answer.

2. Growth is not always beneficial due to the existence of:

   A *Increased unemployment.*
   B *Lower levels of tax revenue.*
   C *Increased fixed costs.*
   D *Increased external costs.*

   Select **one** answer.

3. By increasing output, a firm will increase negative externalities faced by society. This is because by producing more it:

   A incurs higher wage costs.
   B has higher raw material costs.
   C produces more waste.
   D could be left with too much supply.

   Select **one** answer.

ResultsPlus
Build Better Answers

Pollution and the use of non-renewable resources are **two** drawbacks of economic growth. Which do you think is more serious and why? (6)

Think: What problems are caused by pollution? What problems are caused by non-renewable resources? How easy or not is it to deal with these problems? How will they affect people now and in future? Which is more serious and why?

🟥 **Basic** States which is most serious supported by a statement, such as 'Non renewable resources are the most serious because once they have gone they have gone for good.' (1-2)

🟠 **Good** Judgement is made with a supporting statement. For example, 'Pollution would be the most serious drawback of economic growth. Pollution can damage rivers, affecting drinking water. Pollution of the atmosphere can affect the air we breathe and lead to illness. Noise and traffic pollution damage our standard of living. (3-4)

🔺 **Excellent** Judgement is made with supporting justification. For example, 'Pollution would be the most serious drawback, but it depends on certain factors. Pollution creates many problems today. These include damage to drinking water, the destruction of wildlife, smoke and fumes in the atmosphere and traffic congestion. It may also affect future generations if it leads to damage to the ozone later and melting of polar icecaps. Use of non-renewable resources is also a problem. But it may be possible to plant new trees or find alternative power sources such as wind power to use instead so this is a problem that can be solved relatively easily. Persuading people to control and prevent pollution could be far more difficult and expensive, especially as many new countries like China and India are growing so quickly.' (5-6)

Over to you

In 2008 the Daily Mail newspaper started a campaign to 'ban the bag'. Its aim was to stop supermarkets and other shops giving away free single use plastic carrier bags. In order to get the public to support its campaign it published pictures of animals becoming entangled in plastic, the most famous of which was a turtle swimming with the handle of a carrier bag around its neck.

The paper claimed that plastic carrier bags kill over 100,000 marine animals per year and that they damage the environment because they take over 1,000 years to break down in land fill sites. The crude oil that is used to produce the bags is also a non-renewable resource. Almost as soon as the campaign started, Marks and Spencer started charging 5p per carrier bag, and usage dropped dramatically. Pressure was then put on other supermarkets to follow Marks and Spencer's lead. However scientists have since claimed that the Daily Mail's figures were over-exaggerated and the damage done to the environment through plastic bag waste is small, compared to other forms of pollution.

Data show that plastic bags only account for 0.3% of all waste, and that the packaging of supermarket food is far more damaging to the environment than plastic bags. The major supermarket chains of Asda, Tesco, Morrisons and Sainsbury all refused to join Marks and Spencer's decision to charge for bags. As a result the number of single use bags given out barely fell.

Source: adapted from
http://www.timesonline.co.uk/tol/news/environment/article3508263

1. Identify **two** problems that arise from the production or use of plastic carrier bags. (2)

2. Explain how the two problems that you identified in question 1 (above) cause society to incur negative externalities. (6)

3. Using the evidence, evaluate the effectiveness of charging for single use carrier bags as a way of reducing negative externalities. (8)

17 Can growth be sustainable?

Case Study

The remote island of Lewis in the Outer Hebrides is at the centre of a storm. Developers want to build Europe's largest wind farm by erecting more than 230 windmills on peat moor land to the north west of the island. The company behind the scheme, Lewis Wind Power, expect the wind farm to generate enough electricity to power almost half a million homes. The scheme has the backing of the local council and local businesses since it is expected to create 400 jobs and around £6 million per year of benefits to the local community. Some environmental groups are also backing the proposal since generating more electricity from renewables would reduce the use of non-renewable resources. It will also reduce the quantity of greenhouse gases in the atmosphere, reducing the speed of climate change. However, not everybody is in favour of the plans. Local farmers are worried about the loss of grazing land, whilst others are concerned about the impact the wind farms will have on the rare species of bird that nest on the island such as the Golden Eagle.

Objectives

- To understand the concept of sustainable growth.
- To explain the drawbacks and benefits of using renewable resources.
- To understand the ways in which businesses can become more socially, environmentally and ethically responsible.
- To explain why businesses adopt ethical, social and environmentally friendly policies.

edexcel key terms

Sustainable economic growth (development) – an increase in GDP that minimises negative externalities faced by future generations.

Renewable resources – resources that are not limited in supply and are naturally replaced in the environment. e.g. solar power and wind power.

Can growth be sustainable?

Sustainable growth refers to generating economic growth that does not create problems for future generations. The scheme proposed by Lewis Wind Power is an example of **sustainable economic growth**. The aim is to use **renewable resources** such as wind power to generate electricity. Using wind power means that pollution such as carbon emissions, which arise from traditional gas or coal fired power stations, is reduced. Wind power does not require the burning of fossil fuels and so does not use up finite resources but generates electricity which people need to use to heat homes and power business. Wind power can mean benefits are gained without creating problems for future generations. Therefore, negative externalities would be smaller.

As with many economic decisions, there are always going to be some costs to consider. On the island of Lewis, the proposal to build a wind farm was rejected by the Scottish Government in 2008 after it received over 11,000 objections. Most people complained about the effect on wildlife, the noise pollution from the rotating blades and how the ugly wind turbines would destroy the undeveloped beauty of the Outer Hebrides. Therefore, although using renewable resources is a clear solution to the problem of meeting our energy needs without polluting the atmosphere, other local stakeholders can sometimes block plans that benefit the country or planet as a whole. In making a decision on whether to allow such projects to go ahead, the authorities will have to consider the trade-off or opportunity costs that are involved. Are the benefits that would arise from allowing the wind farm to go ahead greater than the loss of the benefits as a result of its development, such as damaging the eco-system, the noise pollution and destroying the natural beauty of an area?

What role does business have?

In order for growth to be sustainable firms have to minimise the negative externalities they create when they produce more output. This could involve cutting down on the amount of noise their factory makes, or agreeing to purchase more electricity that has come from renewable resources. It could even involve reducing the amount of waste or pollution that comes from their production process or finding more creative ways to use the waste and pollution.

For example, in Kent, glasshouses have been built to produce salad crops. The size of the glasshouses is astonishing - seven glasshouses covering an area the size of 39 football pitches. The cost of building the glasshouses was around £80 million. Growing tomatoes and peppers all year round in the UK is not something that we have the natural climate for. The glasshouses have to be heated and the plants have to have the right amount of light and water to produce good crops. However, the developers have designed the site so that it is able to generate its own energy and feed surplus electricity back into the National Grid; it has built reservoirs and has a system to collect rainwater from the roofs of the houses to use to irrigate the plants. Seven reservoirs will be able to hold 65 million gallons of water.

The problem is that finding ways to make better use of resources can involve extra costs to the business. Energy from renewable sources is often more expensive than that produced using non-renewable fuels and reducing pollution and waste or finding ways to re-cycle it usually involves a large investment in expensive technology. Costs will therefore rise, reducing profits. There is a trade-off to consider.

The concern over the costs of economic development has meant that there is now increasing pressure on firms to demonstrate that they are aware of the effect of their operations on the environment. Many firms are now keen to demonstrate that they are taking their responsibilities for their actions more seriously. This is called **corporate social responsibility** (CSR). This involves businesses viewing groups other than just shareholders as important to their success. However, some people would argue this is simply because treating their stakeholders more fairly improves the brand image of the company, allowing it to add value and charge more for its products. Tesco is an example of a company that has been criticised in this way. Some campaigners have argued that its products have too much packaging and the company creates too much waste. There are also concerns about the amount of food miles Tesco uses. This is the distance each item has to travel to reach the shelves of a Tesco store. The longer the distance the more pollution is generated in transporting the food. For example, UK citizens are now able to enjoy a variety of different fruits all year round. However, some of this fruit will travel many miles and use valuable resources to get to us. Strawberries may be great to eat in January but is the cost involved of shipping them from Chile in South America worth it? Again, there is a trade-off.

Tesco has responded to some of this criticism by offering extra Clubcard points to customers who re-used carrier bags and they have erected windmills in some of their car parks to generate more renewable energy. Friends of the Earth argue that this is simply a case of **greenwash** and that Tesco are not doing much to help stakeholders, they are just making it look as though they are to avoid bad publicity and possible new laws that could reduce their profits.

Friends of the Earth believe companies like Tesco can do much more to become 'green' or **environmentally friendly**. Other companies take this a step further and aim to develop **ethical responsibility**. Lush Cosmetics is a company that sees ethical responsibility as an important goal that is central to the business's existence. It only uses natural organic ingredients for its products and does no testing on animals. It also deliberately minimises packaging. Its soap is produced in large cakes and customers have to slice off the amount they want to buy. It also

> **ResultsPlus**
> **Watch Out!**
>
> Sustainable economic growth is not growth that stays constant and does not fall. It is growth where negative externalities are minimised so that the quality of life does not fall for future generations.

edexcel key terms

Corporate social responsibility – a measure of the impact that a business has on society and the environment as a result of its operations

Greenwash – where a business tries to give the impression that it is environmentally friendly when its claims may not be entirely true or justified.

Ethical responsibility – where a business takes a moral standpoint and ensures that its behaviour does not impact stakeholder groups in a negative way; it tries to do the 'right thing'.

Environmentally friendly – where a business acts or produces products in a way that minimises damage to the environment.

donates all of its profits to charities which aim to create a cleaner, fairer world. In this case, Lush is considering all of its stakeholder groups and is trying its best to minimise the negative externalities that the business creates. By doing this, Lush is helping the economy to grow in a sustainable way.

Summary

The problems faced by rapid economic growth across the planet put huge pressure on the environment. In different countries of the world, there are problems with non-renewable resources running out, damage to eco-systems, noise, air, land and water pollution, waste disposal, congestion, climate change and the effect on wildlife and human existence. These are all the costs of economic growth. However, few would argue that the need for economic growth to improve standards of living and quality of life is not a goal that should be targeted.

The big challenge for governments across the world and for businesses is to find ways of achieving growth but where that growth minimises the impact on the planet that we all rely on for our existence. It could well be the case that the next 'revolution' will be in the ways in which government and business work together to create more sustainable growth. In the 19th Century there were concerns that human development was such that the production of food would simply not be able to keep pace and there would be widespread starvation and death. Technological change, invention and innovation helped to avoid such problems but the planet is now faced with a similar dilemma. The trade-offs that are made in the next twenty years may well prove to be vital in ensuring that the planet is able to support the diversity of life and development that currently exists.

Test yourself

1. Which of the following would be an example of a firm becoming more environmentally friendly?

   A Deciding to reduce the amount of packaging on its products
   B Making sure that costs are kept to a minimum
   C Encouraging consumers to use more of their products
   D Advertising the product to make people aware of how green the product is

   Select **one** answer.

2. In order to become more socially responsible, firms should:

   A ensure that they do not create any negative externalities
   B consider the consumer to be the most important stakeholder
   C consider the local community to be the most important stakeholder
   D make sure they consider all stakeholders

   Select **one** answer.

3. Using solar power is an example of sustainable economic growth because:

   A solar power will never run out
   B solar power creates minimal pollution
   C solar power generates electricity more cheaply
   D solar power will only work in countries where there are higher levels of sunlight

   Select **one** answer.

ResultsPlus
Build Better Answers

(i) Identify **one** way in which a supermarket may become more socially responsible. (1)
(ii) Explain how the method you have identified might affect the supermarket. (3)

🟥 **Basic** Identifies one way, such as buying from ethical suppliers who treat their employees well or using recyclable materials in bags. (1)

🟠 **Good** Identifies one way and offers some explanation about how this might affect a business. For example, 'A business can become more socially responsible by using only ethical suppliers. (1) The business might have to check that suppliers are meeting ethical standards. (1) This could increase costs, however.' (1)

🔺 **Excellent** Identifies one way and offers a developed explanation how this might affect a business. For example, 'A business can become more socially responsible by using only ethical suppliers. (1) This could affect a business in a number of ways. It would need to have an ethical policy to check suppliers' activities against. (1) It may also need to employ or train workers to do this job, which can increase costs. (1) It may take time and be costly to investigate new suppliers that meet the criteria.' (1)

Over to you

Renewable energy still only accounts for less than 20% of the planet's electricity production. However, just outside San Francisco, in an area known as 'The Geysers', the world's largest geo-thermal power plant provides enough electricity to power almost 1 million homes. The principal behind geo-thermal energy is a simple one. The further below ground you go the hotter it gets, therefore why not use these hot rocks to heat water and create steam to power electricity generating turbines? The benefits of this type of renewable energy are that very few negative externalities are created since no fossil fuels need to be burnt and no waste is created. The power plants do not require large areas of land and they are not noisy or harm wildlife in any way. At the Geysers power plant, there are further benefits in that treated sewage is forced into the hot rocks rather than clean water. This reduces river pollution at the same time as making electricity.

The United Kingdom currently has three experimental geothermal sites at Falmouth in Cornwall, Cleethorpes in Lincolnshire and Southampton in Hampshire. Unfortunately, geologists state that the UK has the wrong kind of rocks to allow the exploitation of geothermal power. In Iceland, there are five major geothermal power plants which produce about 26% (2006) of the country's electricity.

Source: adapted from www.geysers.com.

1. Explain why geothermal energy could be considered a renewable resource. (3)

2. Explain how geothermal energy could help create sustainable economic growth. (3)

3. Using the evidence, assess the extent to which geothermal energy and other renewable sources could be the solution to the UK's growing demand for energy? (8)

18 What can Government do?

Case Study

In 2010 the prospective owners of top of the range luxury cars will be hit by a brand new tax. Labelled the 'showroom tax' by many, it is in fact an increase in the Vehicle Excise Duty (VED) or 'road tax' for the first year of the life of a brand new car. The new tax will start in 2010 and the top rate of £950 will only apply to those new cars with the biggest engines and the greatest fuel consumption. As a result, they tend to emit the most carbon dioxide from their exhaust, a gas which contributes to global warming and climate change. Cars that emit very little carbon dioxide per kilometre (less than 100g per km) are exempt from the tax and their owners pay nothing. However, even the smallest petrol powered car does not meet this standard, including the 0.7 litre petrol engine Smart Car.

Objectives

- To understand what is meant by tax, subsidy, legislation and regulation.
- To explain how these measures can be used by the Government to protect the environment.
- To appreciate the differences between the various measures the Government uses to reduce pollution.
- To examine the effects these government measures have on businesses.

edexcel key terms

Taxation – a payment made to the Government by consumers or firms. It is usually based on spending or incomes.

What measures can the Government take?

One of the main concerns of economics is human behaviour. Many economic issues relate to the fact that humans behave in a way that might create problems. The desire to have a big car which pollutes far more than smaller ones might be seen as 'bad' behaviour that needs changing. Economists know that to change behaviour, various strategies can be used. People can be punished for behaving in a 'wrong' way or they can be given incentives to change their behaviour to a way that is considered 'better'. This means that governments may have to identify economic activity which is 'bad' (not desirable for some reason) or 'good', (something that is desirable).

There are four key tools that governments use to change behaviour.

- **Taxes**. Imposing a tax on the purchase of a good or service raises its price. When price rises, demand falls. Taxes can be used to reduce demand for products considered 'bad'.
- **Subsidies**. Subsidies are the opposite of a tax. Subsidies are a sum of money given to businesses and other organisations to help them reduce the cost of producing something considered 'good'. If businesses get a subsidy there is an incentive for them to produce more.
- **Legislation**. Legislation refers to laws passed by the government. Legislation can be used to ban or restrict the production of something considered 'bad'. Those who break the law may risk fines, imprisonment and other sanctions.
- **Regulation** Regulation refers to a set of rules that govern the way something is carried out. A body may be set up to monitor an industry with the powers to take action against businesses that break the rules. Some industries are allowed to self regulate - to monitor their own behaviour. If they do not do a proper job then the Government can always step in and set up an independent body. It is in the industries' interests, therefore to make sure they do regulate their own behaviour.

By increasing the rate of VED on the most polluting cars the Government is using **taxation** as a way of getting people to change their behaviour. The aim of the tax is to get the drivers of large, heavily polluting cars to consider the damage they do to the environment. By charging them a tax, it turns an external cost (the pollution they create), which they would not have thought about or have to pay for, into an extra private cost which they do consider since they have to pay it using their own money. This is called **internalising an externality**. By doing this, the aim is to reduce the demand for these types of car and encourage people to buy smaller, more environmentally friendly vehicles. Therefore, taxation can create **incentives** for people to change their behaviour.

However the extent to which behaviour is changed and demand falls depends on how price sensitive the demand for the product is. Many critics argue that the new 'showroom tax' is too small since a person who can afford a brand new luxury car priced at more than £100,000 is hardly going to be put off by an extra £950 in tax.

Rather than making goods and services which create negative externalities more expensive through taxation, an alternative is to make environmentally friendly alternatives cheaper through the use of subsidies. To encourage people to use public transport, the Government gives bus and train companies a **subsidy**. The aim here is to pay some of the company's costs, so the firm can offer cheaper fares and run more services, that otherwise would not make a profit, e.g. late night buses. With cheaper fares, demand should increase, resulting in less people using their cars. This results in there being less pollution and less congestion on the roads.

However, the extent to which this works depends on the amount of the subsidy given, whether there are alternative products and services that people see as being better or more convenient (the number of substitutes) and just how far the cost savings are passed on to the consumer. In addition, the subsidy has to be paid for and the money has to come from tax revenue.

Other options to protect the environment involve **legislation** which **bans** products which are the most polluting. For instance, in 2012 the traditional light bulb will be banned across the European Union. By using fluorescent and energy efficient light bulbs, the European Union believes carbon dioxide emissions can be reduced by 3 million tonnes per year. Therefore to force consumers to use the environmentally friendly alternative, they have passed a law to make sure consumers choose this option.

Regulation can also be used by the Government to minimise pollution and encourage environmental friendliness. This might involve limits as to how much pollution a factory can put into the air or a river or it might include rules about how energy efficient new houses have to be. The large supermarkets have already been threatened with regulation in the future if they do not put in place measures to reduce the use of free single use plastic bags.

What are the effects on business?

The main problem businesses face is that extra taxes and regulation cause a business's costs to increase. A firm's costs may rise through the need to purchase new machinery that reduces the amount of pollution that they emit, or it might be through the need to alter their product to meet a stricter environmental regulation or law. Every increase in cost will reduce the profit margin the business makes through selling the product. Therefore the firm has two choices, if it wants to maintain the size of its profit margin.
- Pass the cost increase onto the consumer by raising prices.
- Try and increase efficiency by cutting costs elsewhere.

The first option is likely to be used by a business whose demand is **price insensitive**, since when prices rise, demand hardly falls and revenue will actually increase. This could also be used by business which believes that by making its product less polluting and more environmentally friendly it will make it different to those of rivals. This is called **differentiation** and can be an important source of

ResultsPlus Watch Out!

Subsidies and taxes are not the same. A tax is a payment made to the Government and a subsidy is a payment from the Government. A tax discourages consumption of a product whereas a subsidy encourages it.

---

edexcel key terms

Internalising an externality – where an unconsidered external cost is turned into a considered private cost which is paid in money.

Incentives – measures designed to encourage a person to act in a different way - a way which may be considered preferable or desirable.

Subsidy – a payment to businesses and other organisations from the government to encourage the production of certain products or to make them cheaper for the consumer

Legislation – laws that are introduced by the Government.

Ban – a law that makes the production of a product or other business activity illegal.

Regulation – restrictions and rules placed on business activities, which may be monitored by an independent body or by the industries themselves.

competitive advantage. Differentiation could result in consumers being willing to pay more for the product. Therefore reducing pollution could actually be a way to add value and increase profit margins if done properly.

The second option will be followed by a firm that operates in a very competitive market where demand is very price sensitive. To remain competitive, low prices are needed; therefore wherever possible the firm will try and offset the increased taxation or regulation costs by reducing other costs such as labour and raw materials.

Some firms might actually benefit from the Government's measures to tackle pollution. For instance, firms that install cavity wall insulation have seen a large increase in demand. The Government now offers a one off payment of £2,700 through its 'Warm Front Scheme' to help people claiming state benefits. This is an example of a subsidy given to the consumer to encourage purchase of a 'good' product. This money has to be spent on making their homes more energy efficient. It can be spent on new central heating or better insulation. In this case, the Warm Front Scheme has increased the profits of these firms dramatically and at the time of writing, householders who qualify are on a three month waiting list.

Summary

Whatever the method used by the Government to try and change behaviour, there will be a trade-off. Increasing the tax on any product is not popular. For those who use larger vehicles, they will feel that they are being unfairly treated and the firms who make the vehicles will see their sales fall for the product which is taxed. These represent the 'cost' side of the equation. On the benefit side, the Government will have to look at the value of the benefits that will result. If consumers do look for more fuel efficient and less polluting cars then the environment as a whole will benefit. People may be healthier if there is less pollution, so that the Government does not have to spend so much on treating people with health problems. This means resources can be diverted to other problems. Firms will have an incentive to carry out research and development on producing more efficient vehicles.

In considering these trade-offs, the Government will have to try to calculate the value of the costs and the benefits to be able to arrive at a decision as to whether a trade-off is worth it. If the value of the benefits gained is greater than the loss of benefits as a result of the decision then it can be argued that it is worth doing.

Test yourself

1. Which of the following is the **best** example of 'regulation'?

    A The Government making a payment to encourage the production of a good
    B Firms deciding to increase prices
    C The Government deciding to tax a good to discourage its use
    D The Government introducing a law which limits the amount of pollution

    Select **one** answer.

2. Which of the following will provide households with an incentive to reduce the amount of electricity they use?

    A A subsidy for each household that uses electricity
    B Greater regulation on firms that produce electricity
    C A tax on the amount of electricity used by households
    D Subsidies for firms that produce electricity from renewable sources

    Select **one** answer.

3. Giving bus operators a subsidy will only be effective in reducing traffic congestion if:

    A demand for car travel is price insensitive
    B demand for bus travel is price sensitive
    C demand for bus travel is price insensitive
    D there are no negative externalities involved

    Select **one** answer.

Over to you

The UK is running out of places to put its rubbish. To combat the problem the Government is taxing councils for every tonne of waste they bury in landfill sites. In 2010 this 'landfill tax' is expected to increase to £48 per tonne. In addition to this the Government is setting strict regulations as to how many tonnes of waste councils can put into landfill sites. Exceed the limit allowed and a council is fined £150 per tonne.

The aim of this system of tax and regulation is to encourage local councils to recycle waste. The UK is running out of landfill sites to bury waste and there is increasing concern over the fact that the UK has much lower recycling rates than other European countries. Local councils have already spent large sums of money introducing doorstep recycling schemes and in some cases have reduced the number of times they collect rubbish from once a week to once a fortnight. The aim is to encourage households to compost and recycle rather than throw waste in the bin.

This has not been popular with some members of the public, however. Some people claim that fortnightly collections encourage rats, attracted by the rotting rubbish. Many people also believe that the Government should be trying to reduce the amount of packaging firms use, rather than punishing householders, who do not create the problem in the first place, for throwing rubbish away.

1. Explain how a landfill tax might encourage local councils to improve recycling schemes. (3)

2. Outline **two** possible impacts on householders from the increase in landfill tax. (4)

3. Using the evidence, discuss the extent to which a landfill tax will help reduce the amount of rubbish that households throw away. (8)

ResultsPlus
Exam Question Report

In 2006, the government announced that it would be setting up some tests to see whether road pricing might work. The plans allow cities like Manchester and Birmingham to bring in a system to make drivers pay to use the roads. It was estimated that drivers might pay as much as £1.30 per mile if they chose to travel at peak times of the day.

The aim of the scheme is to try and reduce the externalities that arise from the increase in the number of cars on Britain's roads.

3 (f) Explain **one** possible benefit to a business of a road pricing scheme. (4) (June 2008)

How students answered

Most students (61%) scored poorly (0-1) on this question. These answers either failed to identify any benefit or simply stated one benefit, such as 'less traffic'.

Some students (38%) gained good marks (2-3) on this question.

These answers identified a benefit and explained how it might affect a business. For example, 'there may be less traffic. This could make roads less congested and make deliveries easier and quicker.'

Few students (1%) gained very good marks (4) on this question.

These answers identified a benefit and clearly explained how it might affect a business. For example, 'road pricing can reduce traffic. This would mean less traffic on the road in the local area. A business may find it easier to get deliveries into its shops or factories in Manchester and ensure its deliveries are on time to customers. Road pricing may therefore reduce the financial costs of late deliveries from suppliers and the poor reputation that follows from late deliveries to customers.'

examzone

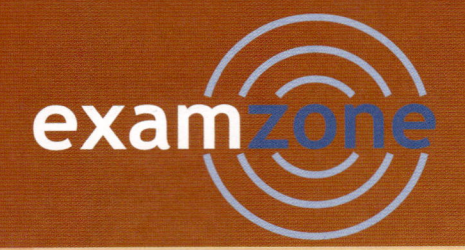

Know Zone: Topic 5.4
Is growth good?

In this topic you have learned about: why economic growth is important and the factors that cause economic growth, how economic growth can lead to an increase in the standard of living, the ways in which a person's standard of living and quality of life can be measured, how economic growth can create problems, specifically the negative externalities of pollution, waste and the use of non-renewable resources, how to make growth more sustainable and the ways in which businesses can become more environmentally friendly, minimising the impacts that they have on the environment, government intervention - what can the government do to protect the environment, why businesses may want to become 'greener' and the problems and the effect that government intervention has on a business.

You should know...

- ☐ The rate of economic growth is measured by looking at the percentage rise in GDP per year.
- ☐ Gross Domestic Product (GDP) is a way of measuring the size of an economy.
- ☐ GDP is the value of all goods and services produced in an economy, normally given over a year or a quarter.
- ☐ Economic growth is generated by investment in machinery, finding new resources, new technology, infrastructure and more productive workers.
- ☐ How economic growth increases living standards.
- ☐ The standard of living refers to the amount of goods and services that can be bought with income.
- ☐ That GDP per capita is a way of measuring the standard of living in a country.
- ☐ Factors such as infant mortality and life expectancy also help you see what the quality of life is like in a country.
- ☐ That growth can have drawbacks and create negative externalities.
- ☐ Negative externalities include waste, pollution, congestion and the use of non-renewable resources.
- ☐ That sustainable growth is economic growth that does not create problems for future generations.
- ☐ That using renewable resources to create sustainable growth can have benefits as well as drawbacks.
- ☐ That many businesses are changing their behaviour to become more environmentally, socially and ethically responsible.
- ☐ That some businesses are trying to appear as though they are environmentally friendly purely to increase profit through 'greenwash'.
- ☐ That the Government can create incentives to reduce the drawbacks of growth.
- ☐ That taxes can be used to make activities that create negative externalities more expensive and thus discourage demand.
- ☐ That subsidies can be used to reduce the price of activities that are environmentally friendly or desirable in some way.
- ☐ That in some cases where the negative externalities are considered so large the Government may have to ban an activity.
- ☐ That the Government action to reduce negative externalities can affect the profit of firms.

Support activity

Write down a list of 5 activities which you or your family have done during a normal week which create negative externalities. Briefly explain what negative externalities are created.

For example, mum drove me into school, causing pollution and traffic congestion.

Then try and put the list in order, starting with the activity which you think created the most serious negative externalities. Use the number 1 to show the activity with the most serious negative externality down to the number 5 which is the least serious. Write a brief explanation of why you have chosen the order you have.

By creating a list and putting your thoughts in order you are actually demonstrating a key examination skill -that of evaluation - By saying which activity is the most damaging and why, you could earn extra marks, rather than just explaining each activity in turn.

Stretch activity

Think about all the activities in your school that create waste, pollution or damage the environment - students and teachers included! In small groups put together a report containing recommendations that you would give to your head teacher or School Council. It should explain what measures your school could take to minimise negative externalities and allow it to become more environmentally responsible. Try to remember that any solution you arrive at will have benefits but also costs. Economists need to consider both before arriving at a judgement. Explain the trade-off in your report and justify your recommendations.

ResultsPlus
Maximise your marks

Plymouth is facing a waste crisis. The city's only landfill site is already full and the Council are paying for the city's waste to be dumped in an old quarry in Cornwall, 15 miles away. However, as the Government gets tough, and has started to fine councils which bury their waste rather than encourage re-cycling, Plymouth City Council has got a new idea - incineration. By burning the waste the council can avoid paying the fines and can create electricity from the heat created. However, few people in Plymouth are keen to have the new incinerator built near them. There are worries about the environmental effects and the extra traffic created.

Source: adapted from www.thisisplymouth.co.uk

(a) Explain why the Government is fining councils who bury large amounts of waste. (3)

(b) (i) Identify two problems for society that might arise if the incinerator is built. (2)

(ii) Explain how the **two** problems you identified in (ii) above create negative externalities. (6)

Student answer

(a) The Government is fining councils who bury large amounts of waste because it wants them to recycle its waste instead.

(b) (i) House prices will fall.
Pollution.

(ii) The incinerator will be smelly and noisy, therefore house prices fall.
Burning rubbish will emit smoke. This smoke might make people ill and could add to global warming. Therefore the environment will suffer an external cost.

Examiner comment

🟥 The student has actually said very little in their answer since virtually all of the answer is a repeat of the question. This is a good example of wasting words and wasting time. The only part of the answer worthy of marks is the mention of recycling therefore only one mark can be awarded.

🟠 In (i) the student has clearly identified two problems. There is no need for any elaboration because the command word in the question is 'identify' Therefore two marks can be awarded.

In (ii), the linked question, there are then up to three further marks for the explanation of each problem. The first suggestion only gains one explanation mark since there is no further development other than 'smelly and noisy'. The second suggestion gets two marks since the smoke is linked to external costs. Therefore this answer would be awarded three marks in total.

Build a better answer

🔺 The first secret to examination success is to look at the command word in the question. In this case the key word is 'explain'. The next step is to look at the marks on offer - in this case three marks. When asked to 'explain' you are being expected to give some development and cover some reasons. A little more detail in the answer will be needed, therefore, to be able to access all the marks.

🔺 To improve the answer in (ii), the student needed to explain the first negative externality in more detail. Perhaps smelly and noisy could have been linked to the area becoming less desirable, which in turn would lead to a fall in the demand for houses, resulting in a falling price. Alternatively, the student could explain why falling house price have led to the owner facing a cost.

Practice Exam Questions

The Severn Estuary between England and Wales has the second largest tidal range in the world. This means that there is a significant difference between the level of water at high tide and the level of water at low tide. Experts believe that the Severn Estuary is one of the best places in the world to generate tidal energy, since it would make use of a key renewable resource. It also has the potential to generate up to 5% of the UK's total electricity needs, reducing the use of conventional power stations that add to global warming. However tidal power is not without its problems. To harness electricity from the River Severn, a 16 kilometre barrage containing 216 turbines would have to be built at an estimated cost of £15 billion. It could also destroy most of the mudflats on the river, which are home to over 75,000 birds.

(a) Outline what is meant by a renewable resource. (2)

(b) (i) Identify **two** stakeholder groups that will be affected if the Severn tidal barrage is built. (2)

(ii) Explain the one effect on each of the two stakeholder groups you identified in (b) (i) above, if the Government decided to build the Severn tidal barrage. (6)

(c) Tidal power is an example of a renewable source of energy. Evaluate whether or not the Severn tidal barrage should be built. (8)

Topic 5.5: Is the world fair?

Topic overview
This topic examines the impact of an increasingly globalised world in creating winners and losers. The role of international trade in raising global living standards is examined as well as the impact it has on less economically developed countries. The question of why countries try to restrict trade is considered, as well as the potential abuse of power by large multi-national companies in less economically developed countries. The issue of poverty is examined, both within the UK and across national boundaries and whether initiatives like Fairtrade and the agreements made to cancel the debt of less economically developed countries have been effective.

Case study
On January 20th 2009 Barack Obama was officially sworn in as President of the United States. He had however, inherited a country in crisis. Unemployment had reached 4.78 million and the US economy was in recession. The new president had a plan to increase the demand for American made goods and services and reduce the number of people unemployed.

The recovery plan involved a package of tax cuts and large scale public spending on projects such as new motorways and wind farms. The package was forecast to cost $819 billion dollars, although many economists are worried that the overall bill could be as high as $850 billion by 2010. In order for the plan to work, the president wanted to make sure that as much money as possible was spent on American made goods and services.

To ensure that this happened and that money was not spent on foreign imports, a law was passed insisting that only American steel could be used in any construction project built as part of the recovery plan. This decision upset both China and Canada, countries which both produce large amounts of steel for the American market. Both countries described the American move as a new form of protectionism and they expected it to result in the loss of large numbers of jobs in their countries. Business leaders in the US were also uncomfortable with the decision to prevent any of the $819 billion being spent on imports. They were worried about how countries like Canada and China would react. Therefore, rather than helping the US economy escape recession, it could actually make it worse.

Source: adapted from http://guizaro5.blogspot.com.

1. What is meant by the phrase 'protectionism'?
2. Why does the US Government want to prevent any of the $819 billion being spent on imports?
3. Why might the decision to restrict spending on imports make the recession worse?

Topic 5.5 Is the world fair?

What will I learn?

Is everybody equal? What is poverty? How does it differ between countries and within a country like the UK? What is the difference between absolute and relative poverty?

Can international trade help? Does international trade benefit a less economically developed country? Have efforts to encourage free trade improved the people's living standards? How can trade be restricted and why would a country want to do this? Do large multinational companies abuse their power in less economically developed countries?

Is there any other help? What can be done to reduce world poverty? What effect have governments, charities and organisations such as Fairtrade had on improving the living standards of people living in less economically developed countries?

How will I be assessed?

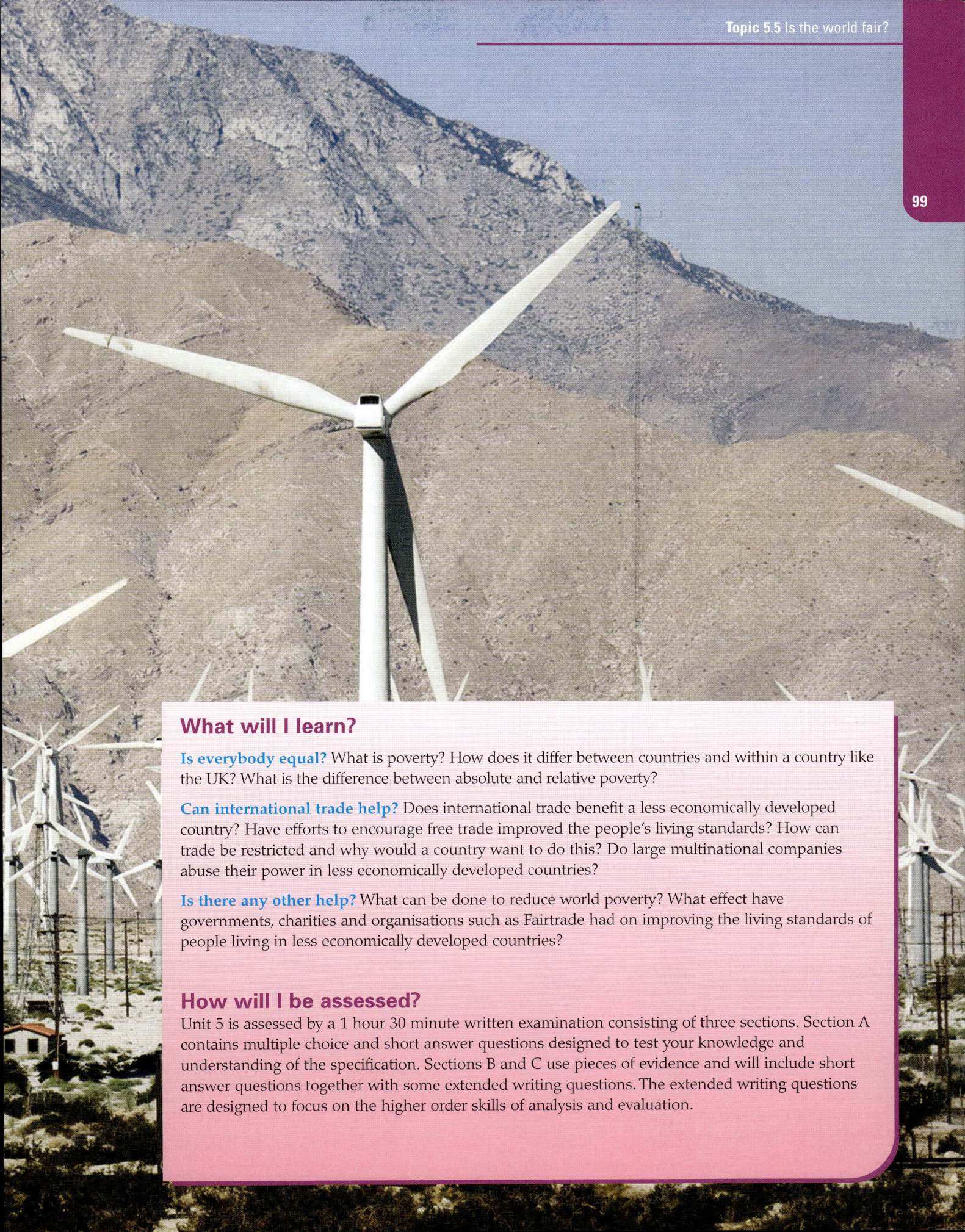

Unit 5 is assessed by a 1 hour 30 minute written examination consisting of three sections. Section A contains multiple choice and short answer questions designed to test your knowledge and understanding of the specification. Sections B and C use pieces of evidence and will include short answer questions together with some extended writing questions. The extended writing questions are designed to focus on the higher order skills of analysis and evaluation.

19 Is everybody equal?

Case Study

In 2007 22% of children living in the UK were officially classed as living in poverty. By 2020 the Government wants to reduce this to zero. It is easy to see why the Government views this as an important objective. According to statistics, if you are one of the 2.9 million children living in poverty, you are likely to have a reading age 2 years behind better-off children by the time you get to secondary school. You are also three times more likely to fail to get 5 GCSE grades at A*-C. This will therefore make it harder for you to get a good job, probably resulting in low income and poverty when you become an adult. However, the poverty faced by children living in the UK is nothing compared to that endured by children in less economically developed countries (LEDCs). In Botswana in Southern Africa, 43% of children do not have access to clean drinking water and only 18% finish primary school. Due to the combination of poverty and AIDS, life expectancy in the country is now below the age of 40.

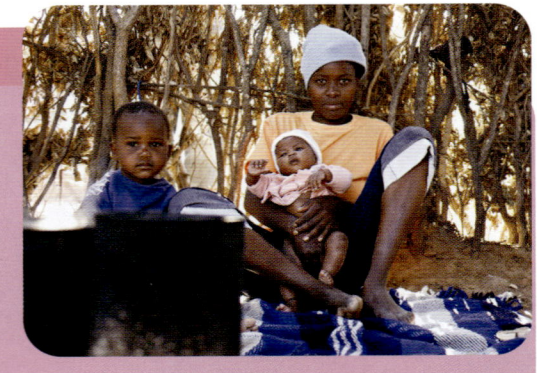

Objectives

- To understand the meaning of the term 'poverty'.
- To appreciate the difference between absolute and relative poverty.
- To identify signs of poverty and inequality in the UK and in LEDCs.
- To use information to make a judgement about a person's standard of living.

edexcel key terms

Poverty line – a level of income usually defined by a government or international body, below which a person would not be able to afford many of the goods and services seen as being the essentials of a decent standard of living.

Welfare state – the system of state benefits and free Government services paid for through taxation. Its aim is to reduce inequality between different groups of people in the UK.

Absolute poverty – where a person cannot afford the basics of life such as food, shelter and clothes.

Universal benefits – payments made by the government to people that are paid regardless of a person's level of income.

Means-tested benefits – payments made by the Government to people which are determined by the amount of income or savings a person has.

Poverty in the UK

There is no one single definition of poverty – it is a relative term. One person's poverty is another person's 'rich'. The World Bank states that a person is living in poverty if they do not have enough income to purchase their basic needs such food, clothing and shelter.

There are two important concepts to understand in relation to poverty.
- Absolute poverty exists where people are unable to afford the basics to support life – food, clothing and shelter.
- Relative poverty exists when a person is unable to access the goods and services that might be considered 'normal' for the people in that country; they may have the basics of life but have few luxuries that ordinary people might take for granted.

In most countries, there is a concept called the **poverty line** which is used to measure the extent to which people in the country live in poverty. In the UK the Government has calculated that a couple with two children aged 5 and 14 needs £346 per week before housing costs in order not to fall below the poverty line.

In the UK, the existence of the **welfare state** has virtually eliminated **absolute poverty**. This is because the Government provides a combination of benefits that boost the incomes of the poor to help prevent the existence of absolute poverty. For instance, every parent is entitled to Child Benefit. This is a **universal benefit** paid by the Government to parents who have children below the age of 16 or who stay in education until the age of 18. In addition to this, the Government also pays out **means-tested benefit** such as Working Tax Credits. These benefits differ from universal benefits in that not everybody qualifies to receive them. They are paid out according to how much income you earn. The more income you earn from work, the less means-tested benefits you will receive.

The Government provides state benefits to allow people on low incomes to purchase basic goods and services, and improve their standard of living. As well as benefits the Government also provides services which are free at the point at which you use them. These public services are paid for through taxation and the aim is to allow the poor access to important services which they would otherwise not be able to afford. These include services such as the National Health Service and education.

The objective of the Government is to try and use the welfare state to prevent large **income inequalities** forming between different groups of people in the UK. Figure 1 demonstrates why there has been a greater focus on reducing poverty in the UK in recent years. Instead of becoming a more equal society, the gap between the rich and the poor has got wider. The graph in Figure 1 shows that in 2007 the richest 20% of the UK population earned 43% of the total income generated in the UK, whereas the poorest fifth of the population earned only 8%.

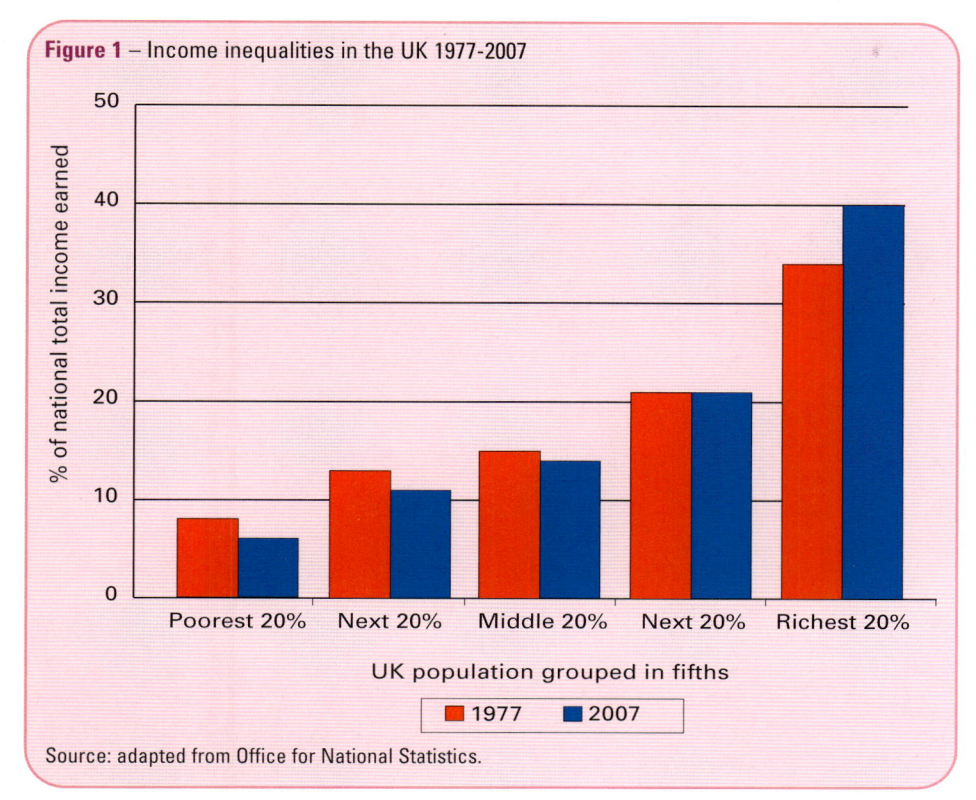

Figure 1 – Income inequalities in the UK 1977-2007

Source: adapted from Office for National Statistics.

Table 1 – Percentage of parents with children who cannot afford selected items in 2008

Item	Percentage
Save £10 per month or more	40
Holiday away from home for one week	38
Replace broken electrical items	22
Money to decorate home	18
Two pairs of shoes for each adult	9
Keep house warm	8

Source: adapted from Department for Work and Pensions, 2008.

ResultsPlus Watch Out!

Absolute poverty and relative poverty are **not** the same. Absolute poverty is where people cannot afford the basics of life such as food, shelter and clothing. Relative poverty is where you have a standard of living which is well below that of an average person in that country. Therefore it is possible to be relatively poor, but not at the same time absolutely poor.

Despite the fact that income inequalities have become wider, the Government has ensured through the welfare state that virtually everybody in the UK has access to the basics of life. As a result, there are few people in the UK who could be described as living in absolute poverty. Therefore the poorest people in the UK tend to face **relative poverty**. This means that those living in relative poverty will be able to afford far fewer goods and services compared to the average person. The data in Table 1 show this by examining the percentage of parents with children who cannot afford certain items. The fact that 22% of people cannot afford to replace their fridge or cooker if it breaks down suggests that the number of people living in relative poverty in the UK is perhaps much higher than people think.

edexcel key terms

Relative poverty – where a person has a standard of living well below the average for that country.

Poverty cycle – where living in poverty makes it harder for you to escape poverty in the long-run.

Poverty in LEDCs

Botswana, on the other hand, is a country that cannot afford a welfare state. As a result, its citizens do not get access to state benefits and there are few Government provided services like a National Health Service. People generally have to look after themselves. Therefore, it is not surprising that children from poor families in Botswana are encouraged by their parents to get a job as quickly as possible. The income each child earns allows the family to afford basics like food, raising their standard of living.

However, without access to a basic education, the chances of getting a job that provides a better income are reduced, making it harder for each child to escape absolute poverty when they reach adulthood. Therefore, it is very difficult for those people living in poverty in Botswana to break out of the **poverty cycle**. This is why many people think that it is important that people in developed nations such as the UK should support charities like Oxfam which raise funds that try and break this cycle. The donations we make to charities like Oxfam are often used on education, tools and machinery to help people break out of the poverty cycle.

Test yourself

1. To escape absolute poverty, a person's income needs to be high enough to afford:

    A food
    B petrol
    C central heating
    D holidays

    Select **one** answer.

2. Which of the following **best** describes the meaning of relative poverty? A situation where a person:

    A has no money
    B does not go to school
    C has few personal possessions
    D cannot afford a foreign holiday

    Select **one** answer.

3. Which of the following is **most likely** to reduce income inequalities between different groups of people in the UK?

    A Universal benefits
    B Means-tested benefits
    C National Health Service
    D State schools

    Select **one** answer.

Over to you

In Brazil, the Government have developed a new scheme to reduce poverty called 'Bolsa Familia' or 'Family Grant'. The scheme pays poor families a benefit of $10 per month for each child attending school, increasing the household income of a typical family living in absolute poverty by 25%. One of the aims of the scheme is to provide an incentive for poor families to keep their children in school rather than encouraging them to find work. It also gives families more money to spend on basic goods and services such as food. Since the introduction of the scheme, income inequalities between the rich and the poor have fallen by 20% and the number of families living in absolute poverty has been reduced by 28%.

Source: adapted from http://www.worldbank.org.

1. (i) State two signs of absolute poverty. (2)
   (ii) Explain how the 'Bolsa Familia' might have led to a 28% reduction in absolute poverty. (3)

2. Explain the reason why the Brazilian Government will only pay the 'Bolsa Familia' benefit to a family if their child attends school. (3)

3. Explain one possible 'opportunity cost' to the Brazilian Government of paying out the 'Bolsa Familia' benefit. (3)

ResultsPlus
Build Better Answers

Pete lives on a run down housing estate. He is unemployed and claims Job Seekers' Allowance and income support. The council provides cheap housing and he uses his benefits to pay for living costs. Pete struggles to afford luxuries.

Explain why Pete is living in relative poverty. (3)

■ **Basic** Simple statement, for example that Pete has less than others. (1)

● **Good** Explains why Pete is living in relative poverty. For example, 'Pete is claiming benefits and lives in cheap housing. It is likely that he will be able to afford fewer goods and services than the average person.' (2)

▲ **Excellent** Defines relative poverty and explains why Pete is living in relative poverty. For example, 'A person lives in relative poverty when he or she has a standard of living well below the average of the country in which he or she lives. Pete is unemployed, claims state benefits and lives in cheap council housing. It is likely that he will be able to afford fewer goods and services than the average person. Pete is therefore likely to have a lower standard of living as a result.' (3)

20 Can international trade help?

Case Study

Nigeria is unique amongst African countries. Not only is it Africa's most populated country with nearly 150 million inhabitants, but it is also the first African country to become almost entirely debt free. By 2006 Nigeria had managed to either repay or negotiate the cancellation of over $30 billion of debt owed to foreign governments. Over the next 15 years it is expected that this will save Nigeria over $47 billion in interest payments alone. This money can now be spent on basic services in an attempt to help the 76% of Nigeria's population which live in absolute poverty. It is also hoped that Nigeria will start to take greater advantage of its huge mineral resources. The country is already Africa's largest oil producer, but the country is also rich in coal, natural gas and a variety of metals. By trading these products internationally, Nigeria will be able to purchase technology from abroad that will allow its industry to develop, boosting its economic growth rate.

Source: adapted from http://allafrica.com/stories.

Objectives

- To understand how trade can bring both benefits and costs to a less economically developed country (LEDC).
- To explain how international trade can lead to improved living standards.
- To understand how free trade agreements, such as the single European market, have increased living standards.
- To examine the reasons and ways in which a country might decide to restrict international trade.
- To consider the costs and benefits of multinational corporations in Less Economically Developed Countries (LEDCs).

edexcel key terms

International trade – the exchange of goods and services between countries.

The benefits of trade

A resource rich country like Nigeria needs **international trade** if it is to experience economic growth and improve the standards of living for its population. International trade allows Nigeria to sell its oil to other countries and use the money it receives to buy the goods and services it needs as well as investing in its own economy; goods such as computers and machinery. International trade also provides an opportunity for countries like Nigeria to concentrate or specialise in producing the goods and services which they have the resources to produce. By concentrating on oil extraction, Nigeria can take advantage of economies of scale which will bring down the cost of extracting each barrel of oil. The more efficient it is in producing oil the more profit it can make from selling its oil. Nigeria can then use the profits from selling the oil to purchase goods that Nigeria cannot make efficiently. Since these countries have specialised as well, the price paid by Nigeria for these goods will be lower.

If countries specialise in the things they can produce best then it can help to enable consumers to have access to products at lower prices. For example, the UK can have access to strawberries all year round because countries that have the right climate for growing this product can produce them and engage in trade. Competition between countries on international markets means that prices are kept low and quality is increased. Therefore, international trade not only improves choice, but it gives the population of a country access to cheaper goods and services. This enables people to buy more with their incomes, improving their standard of living.

The drawbacks of trade

Although international trade brings benefits to a country, it can also bring drawbacks. Nigeria's specialisation in oil extraction means that oil now accounts for 40% of its GDP and 97% of its exports. This is fine when world oil prices are high, but when oil prices fall, Nigeria will not be able to purchase as many goods and services from overseas, reducing standards of living. Sometimes the process of specialisation that international trade encourages can leave a country's economy too dependent on a small number of products and markets. For instance, the African country of Zambia is almost reliant on copper minig for the majority of its GDP.

Figure 1 – Export growth from the EU and the EU GDP per capita

[Bar chart showing % increase with exports and % increase in GDP per capita for years 2004-2007]

Source: adapted from World Trade Organisation.

Table 1 – GDP/ revenues of selected countries/ multinational corporations

Company/Country	Revenues/GDP in $ (Billions)
Greece	360
Wal-Mart Stores (owners of Asda)	351
Shell	319
Denmark	308
BP	274
Nigeria	165
Volkswagen	149

Source: adapted from The World Bank & Fortune Magazine.

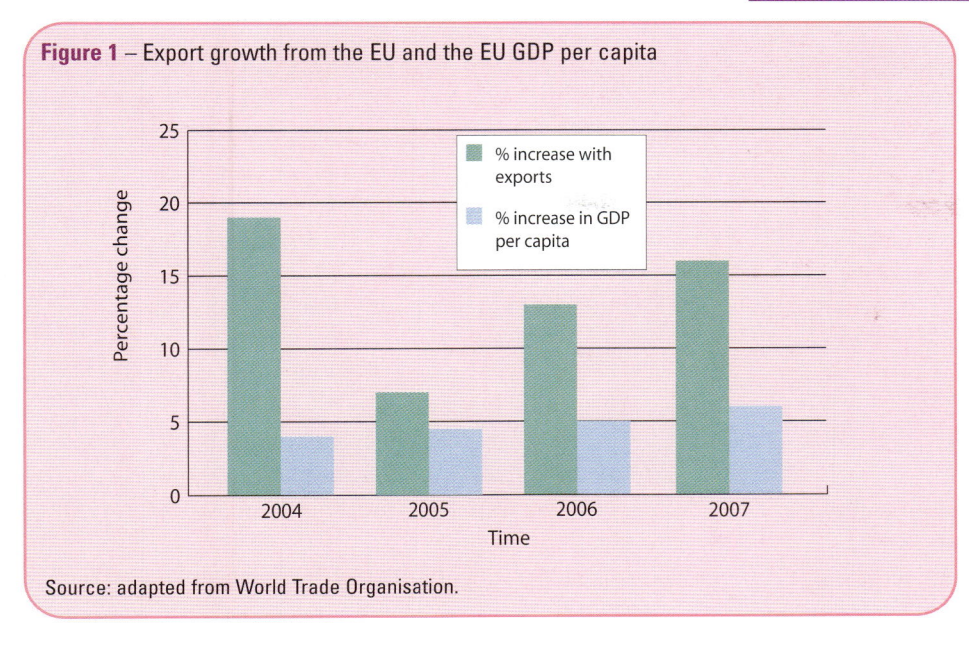

Trade can also create problems with unemployment. Whilst the oil industry is expanding and creating jobs, the textiles industry has declined, as Nigerians choose cheaper foreign imports from Asia over Nigerian produced clothes. The high cost of production in Nigeria, compared to Asia, has made the industry uncompetitive in world markets with over 150,000 people losing their jobs in the last ten years. The fear of large scale job losses and the decline of important industries can at times lead to calls for international trade to be restricted. Whilst this might solve problems in the short-term, it will reduce a country's ability to specialise and force up costs and prices in the long-term, reducing worldwide living standards.

How can trade be restricted?

In order to restrict **free trade**, countries can use a variety of methods.
- **Tariffs** - This is another name for a tax that is placed on imported goods and services. The tax makes foreign imports more expensive, encouraging consumers to buy domestically produced goods and services instead.
- **Quotas** - These are limits to the amount of a particular product that can be imported into a country. If foreign imports are limited, consumers are forced to purchase domestically produced goods and services instead.
- **Non-tariff barriers** - There are many types of non-tariff barriers, but whatever barrier is used the aim is to make it harder for foreign imports to be sold in a country. For instance, imposing strict quality or safety standards on foreign imports might make it more difficult and more expensive for foreign firms to trade with that country. For instance, South Korea prevents oranges from being imported which have a diameter of greater than two inches. This is done to prevent American oranges which are much larger.

The restriction of free trade is sometimes referred to as **protectionism** and countries that use tariffs or quotas often do it to protect an industry or industries which they feel to be under threat from foreign competition. Although this may work in the short-term, in the long-term other countries will retaliate. Why, for example, if Nigeria restricts imports of clothes from China, won't China restrict exports from Nigeria? Therefore, when one country restricts free trade, others tend to retaliate with their own form of protectionism. This then reduces international competition, forces prices up and reduces global living standards.

edexcel key terms

Free trade – the exchange of goods and services between countries where there are no restrictions such tariffs, quotas or other barriers.

Tariff – a tax which is imposed on goods and services which have been imported from abroad and which has the effect of increasing the price.

Quota – a physical limit to the amount of goods and services that can be imported into a country.

Non-tariff barriers – any barriers excluding tariffs that are designed to restrict trade and limit the amount of imports entering a country.

Protectionism – the process of erecting barriers to trade such as tariffs and quotas to restrict the amount of imports coming into a country.

20 Can international trade help?

This is the reason why organisations such as the European Union have helped create a **single European market**. By removing all restrictions to trade within the European Union, EU consumers now have access to greater choice, with a large amount of competition and ability to specialise, forcing prices down and quality up. Therefore, despite not being popular with some people, the free trade that the EU has created within Europe has increased living standards. As restrictions to world trade have been removed the volume of exports has risen. As Figure 1 shows this has a link to improvements in GDP per capita and is one of the reasons why living standards in the EU have risen.

Multinational corporations

As international trade has risen over time, more and more companies have taken the opportunity to sell and manufacture their products in more than one country. The rise of the **multinational** or **transnational corporation** has helped create some very powerful companies which in some cases have more resources than entire countries. Table 1 demonstrates this, with Asda owner Wal-Mart having annual revenues greater than the entire Danish economy.

ResultsPlus Watch Out!

A tariff is not the same as a quota, although they both try to achieve a similar outcome. A tariff taxes a foreign import so that it becomes more expensive. This should then lead to a fall in demand. A quota on the other hand is a limit to the amount of goods and services that can be imported. By reducing the amount of imported goods, this creates excess demand which forces the price of imports up. In both cases the quantity demanded for imports should fall.

edexcel key terms

Single European market – where all restrictions to trade including tariffs, quotas and other barriers have been abolished between countries who are members within the European Union. This has created free trade within the European Union.

Multinational/transnational corporation – a company that is based in one country but manufactures and sells products in a variety of other countries.

Multinational power is at its greatest in LEDCs. In Nigeria, Shell produces over 40% of the country's oil output. However, as you can see in Table 1, Shell has annual revenues that are almost twice the size of the Nigerian economy. This gives Shell large amounts of power over the Nigerian government which gains almost 80% of its tax revenues from oil companies. As a result, some argue that there have been benefits and drawbacks to Nigeria from Shell's multinational operations in the country.

Benefits Some of the possible benefits that have been suggested include the following.
- Shell has invested heavily in the country's ports, pipelines and roads so that oil can be easily exported. These infrastructure improvements have benefited other businesses in Nigeria.
- Shell provides employment to local people, raising local incomes.
- Shell pays taxes to the Nigerian government on every barrel of oil extracted. These tax revenues have helped Nigeria to pay back foreign debt. They now have more money to invest in education and healthcare. This should reduce poverty.

Drawbacks Some of the alleged drawbacks include the following.
- Most of the profit Shell makes from Nigerian oil is sent back to the company's base in Holland, therefore little of it is spent in Nigeria.
- The jobs that are created are usually low-paid, therefore the effect on the local economy is not as big as expected.
- Shell has caused pollution in the Ogoniland region of Nigeria which it has not cleaned up. This has upset the local Ogoni population who have reacted by protesting against Shell, and at times they have forcibly occupied their oil refineries.
- Shell has been accused of socially irresponsible behaviour and possible human rights abuses by providing weapons to the Nigerian police to remove protestors.

Whilst it is clear that multinational corporations do allow LEDCs to improve their economic growth rate, there is also an opportunity for the multinational to exploit its strength, knowing that governments are desperate for the opportunity to gain jobs and tax revenues in order to combat poverty. Therefore the benefits of multinational investment in LEDCs may not be as large as expected.

Source: adapted from www.foei.org/en, www.essentialaction.org/shell

Test yourself

1. International trade can lead to an increase in living standards because:

   A it allows consumers to have a greater choice of goods and services
   B it provides firms with the ability to export goods and services
   C prices for goods and services will decrease
   D imports of goods and services are increased

   Select **one** answer.

2. A tariff restricts international trade because it:

   A increases the price of imported goods and services
   B decreases the price of exported goods and services
   C increases the price of exported goods and services
   D decreases the price of imported goods and services

   Select **one** answer.

3. Multinational corporations can benefit an LEDC because they:

   A make large profits
   B always aim to reduce external costs
   C are always socially responsible
   D help create employment

   Select **one** answer.

Over to you

In 2000 the US Government introduced the African Growth and Opportunity Act (AGOA). Nine years later it has become one of the success stories of international free trade. The scheme's aim was to reduce poverty in West African countries by boosting export demand and making it easier for African firms to trade with the US. The scheme has given 40 West African countries the ability to enjoy the benefits of free trade with the US in over 6,400 different markets from oil to textiles. This involved the removal of all tariff and non-tariff barriers that used to restrict trade between Africa and the US. As a result, AGOA has given African countries a larger market to operate in, where they can take advantage of lower labour costs. In Malawi, the AGOA agreement has led to the creation of over 4,000 jobs in textiles. This in turn has raised incomes and GDP, and has reduced poverty.

Source: adapted from www.agoa.gov.

1. Explain how non-tariff barriers can be used to restrict free trade. (3)

2. Identify **two** reasons why a country such as Malawi will benefit from the AGOA agreement. (2)

3. For each reason identified in Question 2 above, explain how Malawi will benefit. (6)

ResultsPlus Build Better Answers

(i) Identify **one** benefit of a multinational company. (1)

(ii) Explain how the benefit you have identified in (i) might affect a less economically developed country. (3)

Think: What is a multinational company? How do the operations of a multinational affect the country it is operating in and the home country of the multinational?

🟥 **Basic** Identification of a benefit, such as creating employment. (1)

🟠 **Good** Identification of a benefit with some explanation of its effects. For example, 'Creating employment might lead to higher incomes for the local people who work for the multinational.' (2)

🔺 **Excellent** Identification of a benefit with clear explanation of its effects. For example, 'Creating employment might lead to higher incomes. If people from the less economically developed country get jobs with the company they may have higher incomes. This could increase spending in the economy, leading to businesses developing and an increase in the standard of living. However, some of the increased spending may be on imported goods to the country, benefiting businesses outside the less economically developed country.' (4)

21 Is there any other help?

Case Study

In 2005 Comic Relief's Red Nose Day raised £37 million to help people in Africa escape absolute poverty. However this sum is dwarfed by the £28 million African countries pay to the rich 'developed world' nations in interest and debt repayments every single day. In the 1960s and 70s, many poor countries took out loans from developed nations and from international institutions like the World Bank to help them get out of poverty. Often the money was not used appropriately but these countries are suffering the consequences of the borrowing. They have to pay the loans back and also the interest on the loans.

The situation is worse in so-called Heavily Indebted Poor Countries (HIPC). The African country of Malawi is one example of a HIPC, and up until 2006 it was paying over $70 million per year, just in debt repayments and interest. This amounts to almost a third of the Malawian Government's annual budget. Servicing debts owed to rich nations and the World Bank has created large problems in Malawi. Only 58% of the population can read and write, and 60% of the population live below the poverty line on less than 60p per day. The country is also on the verge of famine, and the African AIDS epidemic has infected almost 16% of the Malawian population. More than ever before, Malawi needs foreign help if it is to improve the quality of life for its citizens.

Source: adapted from http://www.jubileedebtcampaign.org.uk

Objectives

- To understand how foreign debt creates poverty in LEDCs.
- To explain how cancelling debt can improve living standards in LEDCs.
- To understand why developed countries have not cancelled more debt.
- To examine the role Non-Governmental Organisations (NGOs), such as charities play in reducing poverty in LEDCs.

edexcel ::: key terms

International debt – a sum of money which is owed by the Government of an LEDC to richer developed nations or organisations such as the World Bank.

World Bank – an organisation that provides loans to LEDCs. It is based in Washington, USA.

Why is debt a problem?

The *international debt* owed by less developed countries has been described by some people as 'modern day slavery'. This is because interest and loan repayments reduce the amount of money left over that can be spent on basic services which can help a country escape the poverty cycle. In the case of Malawi, if the Government did not have to pay £70 million per year to foreign countries and the World Bank, the country would be able to invest more money in infrastructure. This would give more people access to clean running water and basic sanitation, reducing disease.

Government spending on education and healthcare could also be increased. In the long-term this would reduce the spread of AIDS and other diseases like malaria. This would give people living in Malawi the opportunity to get better jobs, increasing incomes and GDP. As a result, the opportunity costs of repaying third world debt are large and in Malawi can usually be measured by the number of people who have lost their lives unnecessarily through extreme poverty. Therefore, the reduction of the debt burden remains one of the biggest obstacles to overcome, if the citizens of LEDCs are to improve both their standard and quality of living.

> 'A lot of the poorest countries are still paying more servicing debts than they do on education and healthcare together. That's unacceptable. Health, and particularly AIDS and malaria have set back economic development 20 years. There's no point cancelling debt if there's no one left alive to benefit.'
> U2 singer Bono during an interview with CNN

Source: http://archives.cnn.com/2002.

What can Governments do?

Many governments and organisations such as the *World Bank* are committed to either reducing or cancelling debt. However, before they are willing to do this, they need to be sure that the cancellation of debt will lead to the extra money being spent on essential government services, such as education, that will reduce poverty rather than on wars or non-essential government projects.

In order to qualify for **debt relief**, countries have first got to prove that they cannot afford to repay the current levels of debt that they have. They then need to demonstrate that they will not run up large foreign debts in the future. Once they have done this they can qualify for debt relief, which involves reducing or cancelling the amount of debt a country owes to its creditors. Malawi benefited from debt relief in 2006, with the World Bank and developed nations cancelling more than $3.1 Billion of debt. This single act reduced annual interest payments from $70 million to around $5million per year. This enabled Malawi to invest in basic services and the extra $65 million released is now being spent on clean water supplies, hospitals and new schools.

In the UK, the decision to cancel debt will cost the UK taxpayer £530 million over the next ten years. Some people argue that the Government should not cancel these debts since the repayments will benefit the UK economy. However, the Government believes that for a rich country like the UK £53 million per year over the next ten years is a small price to pay to reduce almost unimaginable suffering in LEDCs.

Although international debt relief is considered a major method of reducing world poverty, there are other methods available to governments too.

Encourage diversified industry The aim is to make the LEDC less dependent on one product or market, e.g. the country of Zambia relies heavily on copper production for a large part of its GDP. When copper prices fall, the amount of tax revenues the Government earns also falls, resulting in less spending on basic services. Having a greater variety of industries can prevent this problem from occurring.

Encourage investment By improving machinery and factories in a LEDC the productivity of the country's industry should rise. This will cause the unit costs of production to fall, which gives businesses the ability to sell their products at lower prices. This will make exports more competitive, allowing them to be sold in a greater number of markets. Having cheaper domestically produced goods also reduces demand for imports, helping to boost the country's economy.

Limit population growth By actively trying to prevent a larger population, the country's resources will be divided up amongst fewer people. This allows the Government to increase its spending on education and health care for each person.

Encourage free trade By removing barriers to trade, other countries could follow suit. Access to more markets abroad provides an LEDC with the opportunity to export more, improving levels of GDP and taxation revenue. The strategy is encouraged by several Non-Governmental Organisations (NGOs), such as the World Trade Organisation (WTO).

The role of charities and NGOs

Charities and other **Non-Government Organisations** (NGOs) also play an important role in helping to reduce world poverty. The issue of debt has been made topical by the 'Jubilee Debt' and 'Make Poverty History' campaigns. By attracting popular public support they have successfully convinced countries such as the UK to either reduce or cancel debt altogether.

One of the main problems facing poor countries in escaping from poverty is the difficulties they face in competing on world markets. Countries like Malawi tend to have one major product to export. In Malawi one of their main exports is sugar; in

> **ResultsPlus Watch Out!**
> Debt relief does not necessarily mean that debt is cancelled. Debt relief can include a reduction in the amount of money owed to the World Bank or the Governments of developed nations as well as a complete cancellation of the debt that is owed.

> **edexcel key terms**
> **Debt relief** – the reduction or cancellation of debt that LEDCs owe to either the World Bank or developed nations.
> **Charities** – organisations that aim to produce a surplus of income over expenses to promote a good cause.
> **Non-Government Organisations** – independent non-profit organisations that aim to achieve a particular objective, e.g. debt cancellation.

21 Is there any other help?

Figure 1 – The Fairtrade Foundation

The Fairtrade Foundation states that Fairtrade is about: '... better prices, decent working conditions, local sustainability, and fair terms of trade for farmers and workers in the developing world. By requiring companies to pay sustainable prices (which must never fall lower than the market price), Fairtrade addresses the injustices of conventional trade, which traditionally discriminates against the poorest, weakest producers. It enables them to improve their position and have more control over their lives.'

Source: http://www.fairtrade.org.uk/what_is_fairtrade/faqs.aspx

Mali, cotton is the major export. The problem is that many developed counties have trade barriers in place which make it difficult for them to sell their products and get a fair price. For example, the United States also grows cotton and the US government provides over £2 billion in subsidies to cotton farmers. This makes it cheaper for US growers to produce cotton and keeps farmers and workers in the US in employment but also drives down the price of cotton as supply is increased.

However, the growers in countries like Mali, Benin and Burkina Faso do not have these subsidies. Around 10 million people in Africa depend on cotton for their livelihoods. For buyers of cotton, buying cheap US cotton is a better option than the more expensive Mali cotton. The result is that African cotton producers find it difficult to compete and earn a living given that prices are relatively low.

One of the solutions would be to reduce subsidies on US cotton and this is something that is being addressed. However, there is a trade off. There should be benefits to African growers of the reduction in cotton subsidies but the action may well mean that US farmers and workers lose their jobs and livelihoods.

World Trade Organisation International institutions such as the **World Trade Organisation** (WTO) are trying to help open up markets across the world to promote free trade. By promoting free trade across nations, the WTO is trying to encourage countries to remove tariff and non-tariff barriers that prevent LEDCs competing in international markets. The task is a very complex one with countries throughout the world wanting to boost their own position but not always being willing to make sacrifices for the benefit of the world as a whole – the problem is one of trade offs. The European Union, for example, has refused to remove barriers which will allow Malawian Sugar to be imported. The European sugar market is estimated to be worth $32million per year to Malawi, but without access to markets, Malawi is missing out on revenue that could be boosting its economic growth rate and raising the standard of living.

Fairtrade Foundation The **Fairtrade** Foundation is another NGO which is owned in part by charities such as Oxfam and Christian Aid. Its aim is to improve the income levels of farmers in LEDCs by giving them the ability to sell their produce at a higher price than that which exists on world markets.

The existence of Fairtrade reduces the ability for large multinationals to exploit small farmers. By paying a much higher price for agricultural produce like coffee, bananas and cocoa, food producers who use Fairtrade crops can use the Fairtrade label on their packaging. This in turn allows them to charge a higher price in the shops since consumers are willing to pay more for products which are **ethically responsible**. Since farmers in LEDCs now receive a higher income, GDP is increased, raising incomes and living standards amongst the poor.

There have been critics of Fairtrade, however. In February 2008, the Adam Smith Institute, a 'think tank', produced a report that questioned the extent to which Fairtrade did benefit farmers in less developed countries. They argued that whilst some farmers will qualify under the Fairtrade agreement and get some benefits, farmers outside the agreement will be affected by the fact that prices in the market have been distorted. The Institute suggested that only 10% of the extra price that consumers pay for Fairtrade products goes to the farmer – the rest goes to other people in the supply chain. If farmers get protection from Fairtrade they might also not be as willing to look to diversify and invest in new production methods. If this were the case then future generations of farmers in LEDCs will be affected. The Fairtrade Foundation rejects these criticisms.

edexcel key terms

World Trade Organisation – an organisation that aims to promote international free trade.

Fairtrade – an NGO which aims to improve living standards in LEDCs by paying higher prices for agricultural produce.

Ethically responsible – where firms act with a moral sense of responsibility towards their stakeholders.

Over to you

In September 2009, the UK's biggest selling chocolate bar 'Cadbury's Dairy Milk' will start to display the Fairtrade logo for the first time. This groundbreaking move will lead to a tripling of demand for cocoa purchased through the Fairtrade system. In the African country of Ghana, it is expected that this will create large benefits for thousands of cocoa farmers. They will now be able to sell their produce at a higher price because of the premium which is paid by the Fairtrade foundation. It is expected that the Cadbury deal will increase incomes and boost the GDP of Ghana, one of the world's largest cocoa producers. This should in turn reduce the number of people living in absolute poverty.

In 2008 sales of Fairtrade products in the UK exceeded £500 million for the first time. In 1997 they accounted for sales of only £16.7 million. Despite the amazing growth rate during the last ten years, Fairtrade produce still only accounts for a small percentage of the overall grocery sales made in the UK.

Source: adapted from http://www.fairtrade.org.uk.

1. Explain **one** reason why Cadburys might want to buy cocoa through the Fairtrade foundation. (3)

2. Using your knowledge of economics and business, assess the strength of the case for Fairtrade and other NGOs being able to eliminate world poverty. (10)

Test yourself

1. Debt reduces living standards in LEDCs because:

    A a country is forced to increase imports from abroad
    B a country is forced to reduce exports to foreign countries
    C debt repayments reduce spending on health care
    D taxes have to be reduced

    Select **one** answer.

2. The World Trade Organisation can help to reduce poverty by:

    A increasing the number of exports abroad
    B reducing the number of imports into a country
    C restricting free trade
    D promoting global free trade

    Select **one** answer.

3. Fairtrade is most likely to increase the standard of living in LEDCs because:

    A farmers can sell more of their produce
    B farmers get paid a premium for their produce
    C farmers get a guaranteed market abroad
    D the Fairtrade brand is ethically responsible

    Select **one** answer.

ResultsPlus
Build Better Answers

(i) Identify **one** method that governments could use to help less economically developed countries. (1)

(ii) Explain how a less economically developed country might benefit from this method. (3)

🟥 **Basic** Identification of a method such as canceling the debt or debt relief. (1)

🟠 **Good** Identification of a method with some explanation of the benefits. For example, 'Cancelling the debt, or debt relief, would mean that less economically developed countries. would not have to make payments to other countries.' (2)

🔺 **Excellent** Identification of a benefit with clear explanation of its effects. For example, 'Cancelling the debt or providing debt relief, would mean that less economically developed countries would not have to make payments to other countries. They would also not have to pay the high levels of interest on loans. As a result they would retain more money in the country. This could be spent on programmes to help improve education and health care, as well as developing roads and transport. These programmes could help the country to experience economic growth.' (4)

examzone

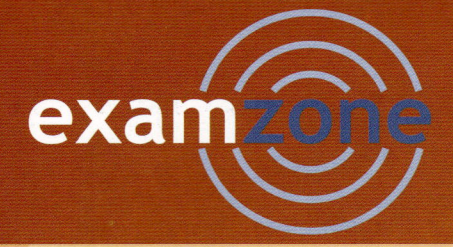

Know Zone: Topic 5.5
Is the world fair?

In this topic you have learned about: how poverty can vary from country to country, the difference between absolute and relative poverty, how the UK uses benefits to reduce income inequalities, why trade is important and how international trade can create both costs and benefits, how free trade can lead to improvements in the standard of living, the various ways in which trade can be restricted including tariff and non-tariff barriers, the costs and benefits of multinational corporations for LEDCs, how the cancellation of debt can reduce poverty in LEDCs and what charities and other organisations are doing to help reduce international poverty.

You should know…

- [ ] Income inequalities are the difference between the incomes of different groups of people.
- [ ] The Government can reduce income inequalities by using benefits which boost the incomes of the poorest people in the country.
- [ ] The existence of benefits and the provision of important services such as the NHS have virtually eliminated absolute poverty in the UK.
- [ ] Poverty in the UK tends to be relative, unlike poverty in parts of Africa which tends to be absolute.
- [ ] International trade reduces the prices of goods and services, which increases the standard of living.
- [ ] International trade can boost GDP, but can also bring drawbacks.
- [ ] How tariffs, quotas and other barriers can be used to restrict international trade.
- [ ] The reasons why countries might want to restrict international trade.
- [ ] The benefits and drawbacks multinational corporations can bring by investing in LEDCs.
- [ ] Reducing or cancelling debt has reduced the amount of absolute poverty in LEDCs.
- [ ] There are other methods by which governments can reduce world poverty.
- [ ] The cancellation of debt will have a minimal impact on the standard of living of many people in developed countries, but will have a large impact on the standard of living of people living in LEDCs.
- [ ] Promoting free trade can also boost economic growth in LEDCs.
- [ ] How Fairtrade has boosted the incomes of people living in LEDCs.

Support activity

Go online and choose a multinational company to research. On many companies' websites there will be a page explaining what the company is doing to ensure that they are operating in a socially responsible way. Firms can sometimes refer to social responsibility as 'corporate social responsibility'. To find the social responsibility web page you may need to use the 'search' function on the company's homepage.

In small groups design a three minute presentation which explains what your chosen company is doing to be socially responsible. In your presentation consider whether the company actually wants to be responsible or is using it as a way of deflecting criticism over its activities or as a way of marketing its products.

Stretch activity

Discuss whether your school might want to become a Fairtrade school. To become a Fairtrade School you will need to set up a steering group to manage the project and complete the application form. This can be downloaded from www.fairtrade.org.uk/schools.

ResultsPlus
Maximise your marks

Before obtaining debt relief, the citizens of Zambia had very few options if they became sick. The only way of getting medical help was to visit a private doctor and that often cost more than twice what the average Zambian earns in a day. With 65% of the country's population living in absolute poverty, it was unsurprising that many people died from their illnesses through a basic inability to afford medical treatment. In 2006 Zambia secured $4 billion of debt relief from the World Bank. This has allowed the Government to increase spending on health care. Clinics and hospitals now offer free treatment to all. However this improvement highlighted another of the country's problems, the country only has one doctor for every 14,000 people.

Source: adapted from www.oxfam.org/en/news/pressreleases2006/pr060331_zambia.

(a) The average Zambian earns less than $1 per day. Identify **two** problems that this may cause for a person living in such a country. (2)

(b) Better health care and better education are **two** ways of eliminating absolute poverty in Zambia. Which do you think would be the most effective and why? (6)

Student answer

(a) Cannot afford to buy lots of food, therefore they will feel hungry and starve. They also might not be able to afford to go to school so they will not be able to get an education and get a job.

(b) Better health care is the most important way of removing absolute poverty, since if you are ill, you cannot work and if you cannot work you will receive no income which means you can't buy things like food which you need to help escape absolute poverty. The Zambian Government can't afford to pay benefits so you will probably die if you get sick.

Examiner comment

🔴 The student has identified two problems that are created through extremely low incomes, and will therefore score two marks. However the question is asking you to 'identify' two problems. Therefore no marks can be awarded for any of the development the student has built into their answer.

🔴 The question stem states two ways of eliminating absolute poverty in Zambia. To create an answer which scores all six marks, you have to make a judgement about which is the most important and explain why. However to go beyond four marks you must refer to both of the ways suggested in the question stem, i.e. 'health care' and 'better education'.

The student has made a judgement that health care is the most important way to reduce absolute poverty and has explained the reasons why in lots of detail. Excellent terminology and links between ideas are also evident. However there is no reference in the answer to 'better education' limiting the score to four out of the six marks available.

Build a better answer

🔺 The student has scored all of the marks available, but has ignored the command word in the question. The question requires the identification of two problems and does not require any explanation or further development. Therefore, the student could have attained full marks by simply writing:

'cannot afford health care and cannot afford to get an education'.

Over-explaining answers when the command word in the question does not require it can be expensive. If this approach was repeated across the paper it might prevent the student finishing the exam paper which might affect the grade they perhaps deserve.

🔺 To improve the answer the student could have left out the final sentence about the Zambian Government not paying benefits. This could have been replaced by 'However education is also important in the long-term. If you cannot read or write you will not be able to get a job and gain an income. Therefore health care is important immediately, but education will also be important later on'. The use of the word 'however' shows the examiner that you are likely to be writing an evaluative response.

Practice Exam Questions

In February 2009 Mercedes Benz, the luxury German car manufacturer, opened its new factory in Pune, India. The factory cost $56 million to build and has created 350 jobs. The factory manufactures cars and trucks, both for the Indian market and for export to other countries in Asia. The success of the export market is dependent on countries such as China lifting trade barriers which limit the number of cars that can be imported. It is expected that the new Mercedes factory will have a large effect on the Pune region. Car workers get paid more than the average wage for the area and Mercedes intends to invest heavily in local schools and in the training of its staff.

Source: adapted from www.benzinsider.com.

(a) Explain one way in which international trade will benefit people in LEDCs. (3)

(b) Explain one reason why some countries might choose to restrict international trade. (3)

(c) Assess the extent to which multinational corporations can help to reduce poverty in LEDCs. (10)

Zone in ● Planning Zone ● Know Zone ● Don't Panic Zone ● Exam Zone ● Zone Out

Welcome to examzone

Revising for your exams can sometimes be a scary prospect. In this section of the book we'll take you through the best way of revising for your exams, step-by-step, to ensure you get the best results that you can achieve.

Zone In!

Have you ever had that same feeling in any activity in your life when a challenging task feels easy, and you feel totally absorbed in the task, without worrying about all the other issues in your life? This is a feeling familiar to many athletes and performers, and is one that they strive hard to recreate in order to perform at their very best. It's a feeling of being 'in the zone'.

On the other hand, we all know what it feels like when our brains start running away with us in pressurised situations and can say lots of unhelpful things like 'I've always been bad at exams', or 'I know I am going to forget everything I thought I knew when I look at the exam paper'.

The good news is that 'being in the zone' can be achieved by taking some steps in advance of the exam. Here are our top tips on getting 'into the zone'.

UNDERSTAND IT
Understand the exam process and what revision you need to do. This will give you confidence but also help you to put things into proportion. These pages are a good place to find some starting pointers for performing well at exams.

DEAL WITH DISTRACTIONS
Think about the issues in your life that may interfere with revision. Write them all down. Then think about how you can deal with each so they don't affect your revision.

FRIENDS AND FAMILY
Make sure that they know when you want to revise and even share your revision plan with them. Help them to understand that you must not get distracted. Set aside quality time with them, when you aren't revising and when you aren't worrying about what you should be doing.

COMPARTMENTALISE
You might not be able to deal with all issues. For example, you may be worried about an ill friend, or just be afraid of the exam. In this case, you can employ a useful technique of putting all of these things into an imagined box in your mind at the start of your revision (or in the exam) and mentally locking it, then opening it again at the end of your revision session.

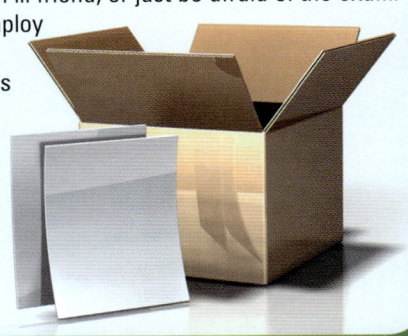

BUILD CONFIDENCE
Use your revision time not just to revise content, but to build your confidence for tackling the examination.

DIET AND EXERCISE
Make sure you eat well and exercise. If your body is not in the right state, how can your mind be?

More on the Active Teach CD

Planning Zone

The key to success in exams and revision often lies in the right planning. Knowing what you need to do and when you need to do it is your best path to a stress-free experience. Here are some top tips in creating a great personal revision plan.

First of all, know your strengths and weaknesses. Go through each topic making a list of how well you think you know the topic. Use your mock examination results and any further tests that are available to you as a check on your self-assessment. This will help you to plan your personal revision effectively by putting a little more time into your weaker areas. Importantly, make sure you do not just identify strengths and weaknesses in your knowledge of the content but also in terms of exam technique – what aspects of the assessment objectives are you weakest on, for example?

Next, create your plan!
Use the guidelines across the page to help you.

Finally, follow the plan!
You can use the sections in the following pages to kick-start your revision and for some great ideas for helping you to revise and remember key points.

More on the Active Teach CD

Cut your revision down into smaller sections. This will make it more manageable and less daunting. In Business Studies and Economics you could follow the order of topics and sub-divisions within topics in the specification, which is clearly divided up already. Revise one at a time, but ensure you give more time to topics that you have identified weaknesses in.

Be realistic in how much time you can devote to your revision, but also make sure you put in enough time. Give yourself regular breaks or different activities to give your life some variance. Revision need not be a prison sentence.

Find out your exam dates. Go to www.edexcel.com to find all final exam dates, and check with your teacher.

Make sure you allow time for assessing progress against your initial self-assessment. Measuring progress will allow you to see and celebrate your improvement and these little victories will build your confidence for the final exam.

Make time for considering how topics interrelate. For example, in Business Studies and Economics, try to see where all the parts of the specification fit together. A business has to deal with lots of things all at once and cannot separate them out easily. You have to show that you are aware of all these factors. For example, a business might plan a marketing strategy but has to take into account the fact that interest rates might change and affect sales or that exchange rates may affect both costs and revenues if the business trades abroad.

Draw up a calendar or list of all the dates from when you can start your revision through to your exams.

Make sure that you know what the assessment objectives against which you will be measured are and what they mean. Get to know the command words that will give you a guide as to what assessment objectives you are expected to demonstrate.

● Zone in ● Planning Zone ● **Know Zone** ● Don't Panic Zone ● Exam Zone ● Zone Out

Know Zone

In this section you'll find some useful suggestions about how to structure your revision for each of the main topics. You might want to skim-read this before starting your revision planning, to help you think about the best way to revise the content. Different people learn in different ways – some remember visually and therefore might want to think about using diagrams and other drawings for their revision. Others remember better through sound or through writing things out. Some people work best alone, whereas others work best when bouncing ideas off friends on the same course. Try to think about what works best for you by trialling a few methods for the first topic.

Remember that each part of the specification could be tested, so revise it all.

Writing revision plans

A useful technique to help you revise important points is to summarise topics into short points. It can be difficult to remember lots of information from textbooks or the notes you have taken during your course. To make notes on a topic:

- read the topic carefully;
- highlight the key points in the topic;
- identify the important information in each point;
- decide how to summarise each point into a short sentence so that it is easy to remember.

Below is an example of how this could be done for Unit 5 - 'What can Government do?' from Topic 5.4.

Topic 5.4 What can Government do?

- Government might identify economic activities which are 'bad' and try to control them or activities which are 'good' and try to promote them.
- Government can affect economic activity by using taxation, subsidies, legislation or regulation.
- Imposing a tax raises the price of a product. Taxation can be used to reduce demand for products the Government thinks are 'bad', by increasing their price.
- Government can use taxes to turn an external cost (that people or businesses would not usually have to be pay, i.e. the cost of pollution) into a private cost (paid from people's or business's own money).
- Turning an external into an internal cost is called internalising an externality. It can be used to give people or businesses an incentive to change their behaviour.
- A subsidy is money given to businesses to help them reduce costs and give them an incentive to produce more and reduce prices.
- Subsidies can be given to business to develop environmentally-friendly products, for example, or to bus or train companies to encourage people to use this form of transport rather than cars.
- Legislation is laws to ban, control or restrict production of goods the Government considers 'bad'.
- The extent to which a subsidy works depends on:
  – the amount given;
  – whether people prefer alternative or substitute products or services;
  – how much of the subsidy is passed on;
  – whether taxation is enough to pay for it.
- Businesses or people that do not abide by legislation may be fined or imprisoned.
- Regulation is setting rules and monitoring business behaviour to make sure they carry out activities in a certain way.
- Regulation may be limits on production or pollution or rules to control business activities.
- Some industries self regulate. They have a body made up of people and businesses in that industry which controls their activities.
- One problem is that taxes and regulation increase costs for businesses.
- If a business wants to maintain profits it might pass on the costs in the form of increased prices. It is likely to do this if demand for its products is price insensitive or because people are prepared to pay a higher price for that type of product.
- If a business wants to maintain profits it could try to cut costs elsewhere by increasing efficiency.
- Some businesses benefit from Government measures. For example, payments to people to encourage them to insulate houses can benefit businesses providing this service.

Memory tips

In the examination you will need to remember important facts, information and data that will help you to answer questions. Some of these will simply be a list of terms such as:

- the types of negative externality;
- the types of taxation in the UK;
- the stakeholders of a business.

Others might be a list of phrases such as:

- the costs of unemployment;
- the drawbacks of trade for a Less Economically Developed Country;
- the effects of low interest rates.

Memory tips - Mnemonics

This is a word that is made up from the first letters of the terms you want to remember. Some well know phrases in business and economics are:

- PESTLE – the Political, Economic, Social, Technological, Legal and Environmental factors affecting a business;
- SWOT – the Strengths, Weaknesses, Opportunities and Threats facing a business;
- the 4 Ps of the marketing mix – Price, Product, Promotion and Place.

You can make up your own mnemonic. For example, to remember the factors affecting demand use the mnemonic IFACT – Income, Fashion, Advertising, Competition, Tastes (try to remember it as 'eye' fact)

Memory tips - Visual presentation

Some people remember if the information is a picture or diagram. An example of a diagram that could be used to remember the internal and external shareholders of a business is shown below.

Internal Stakeholders: Shareholders, Employees, Managers

External Stakeholders: Suppliers, Local Community, Customers, Pressure Groups, Government

More on the Active Teach CD

Know Zone

Memory tips - Mindmaps

A mindmap is a diagram that records words and ideas and shows connections. At the centre of the map, or page, is the main word or idea. Flowing out from this main word or idea is a number of key words and ideas linked to the main word. Mindmaps are used in business. But you can also use a mindmap for your revision. Below is a mindmap outlining economic problems.

Changing demand

AFFECTED BY:
- Incomes
- Fashion
- Advertising
- Competition
- Tastes

Inflation

CAUSED BY:
- Increasing costs
- Rising demand compared to suppy

PROBLEMS:
- Rising cost of living for consumers
- Increasing production costs of materials

Economic problems

Unemployment

COST TO INDIVIDUAL:
- A lower level of income
- Loss of self-esteem
- Loss of skills
- Family break-up

PROBLEMS:
- Government will receive less tax
- Greater need for state benefits
- Crime
- Impact on other businesses

Don't Panic Zone

Once you have completed your revision in your plan, you'll be coming closer and closer to The Big Day. Many students find this the most stressful time and tend to go into panic-mode, either working long hours without really giving their brain a chance to absorb information, or giving up and staring blankly at the wall. Some top tips are shown here.

- Test yourself by relating your knowledge to business issues that arise in the news – can you explain what is happening in these issues and why?

- Get hold of past papers and the mark schemes for the papers. Look carefully at what the mark schemes are expecting of the candidate in relation to the question.

- Get hold of a copy of the Examiner's Report from the previous exam series. It contains lots of useful advice about where candidates performed well and where the main mistakes were. Learn from these. The Examiner's Report and past papers are often available on the awarding body Website – check with your teacher.

- Do plenty of practice papers to hone your technique, help manage your time and build confidence in dealing with different questions.

- Relax the night before your exam – last minute revision for several hours rarely has much additional benefit. A runner doing a marathon is unlikely to practice the night before by going for a quick 15 mile run. Your brain needs to be rested and relaxed to perform at its best.

- Remember the purpose of the exam – it is for you to show the examiner what you have learnt and understood about business. It is not a means of trying to trick you.

Last minute learning tips for Business Studies

The week before the exam should be spent going through past papers. Look at each question carefully and compare question types. Make sure that you are familiar with the different types of question and you know the style needed to answer each question.

There will be **multi choice** questions or **objective test** questions. These ask you to make a choice from a series of options, such as 'Which **one** of the following is an export from the UK?' **or** 'Which of the following is **not** a reason for taxation in the UK? Select **one** answer.'

There will be questions assessing your **knowledge** and **application** skills, such as 'What is meant by the term "stakeholder"?' and 'Identify **two** effects of a strong pound in the passage.'

Certain questions will test **analysis** and **evaluation** such as 'Explain how a fall in interest rates might affect a business' or 'To what extent can pressure groups affect a business? Justify your answer.'

Try to devote some time to actually writing out the answers in the time period allowed to refine your skills. You can check your answers against the mark scheme to see how you would have performed. Make sure you understand what the command words are for each question and how they relate to the assessment objectives. For example, an 8 mark question might consist of 2 marks for knowledge, 2 for application and 4 for analysis and evaluation.

Remember that you can get full marks by answering in the space provided on the exam paper - it is not the amount you write but the quality and the extent to which you demonstrate the assessment objectives being targeted.

On the night before the exam, relax, give your brain a rest and try and do something you enjoy. Get to bed at a reasonable hour so that you can get a good night's sleep and be refreshed for the exam.

More on the Active Teach CD

Exam Zone

What to expect in the exam paper

The assessment for Unit 5 is through an examination which will last for one and a half hours. Students are required to answer all questions. There will be a total of 90 marks. The examination will be divided into three sections which include a variety of questions including:

- multiple choice questions;
- short answer questions;
- extended answer questions.

Sections B and C will consist of questions based on a scenario given in the examination.

Understanding the language of the exam paper

Which of the following is... Select one answer	You need to identify the correct response from a selection of options.
Which two of the following are...	You need to identify the two correct responses from a selection of options.
Which of the following is most likely to...	The key is 'most likely' – this means that there could be more than one option that is possible; you have to decide which is the most likely.
Which of the following is not...	This is a question asking you to spot the negative option from a list – read each option carefully.
Fill in the blanks	This may require you to complete some calculations in a table, for example.
What is meant by...	This requires you to give a definition of a key term in business studies – an example to help support the definition is usually worth giving also.
Identify...	This type of question requires only a one word answer or a short phrase or sentence – it is associated with knowledge and understanding and often requires the student to extract information from a context.
State...	Similar to 'identify' – again usually only requires a one word answer.
Describe...	Give the main characteristics of a topic or issue.
Explain...	Describe the issue, term etc, giving reasons or features.
Analyse...	Break down the topic or issue into manageable parts to help explain what is going on, how something works, what relationships may exist and what assumptions might be made.
Assess...	Offer a judgement on the importance, significance, relevance and value of something, with reasons why you have made such a judgement.
Do you think...	Asking you to make a judgement – which requires support and reasons to be given for the judgement.
What is the most important...	Another question asking you to make a judgement and offer support for the judgement. Explain why one factor is more important than another and why.
To what extent...	Is the issue very, very important/significant/, quite important/significant, moderately important/significant, not very significant/important at all – and why?
Evaluate...	Arrive at a judgement – with some support for your reasoning.
Justify...	Offer support and reasons for the judgement you have made – and why.
Write a report...	A report might consist of advantages and disadvantages, key features, summaries and judgements about the value of one option against others.

Exam Zone

Meet the exam paper

This diagram shows the front cover of the exam paper. These instructions, information and advice will always appear on the front of the paper. It is worth reading it carefully now. Check you understand it. Now is a good opportunity to ask your teacher about anything you are not sure of here.

Print your surname here, and your initial afterwards and sign the paper. This is an additional safeguard to ensure that the exam board awards the marks to the right candidate.

Here will be the school's centre number.

Ensure that you understand exactly how long the examination will last, and plan your time accordingly.

Make sure you are aware of how many marks are given for each question and write to justify these marks.

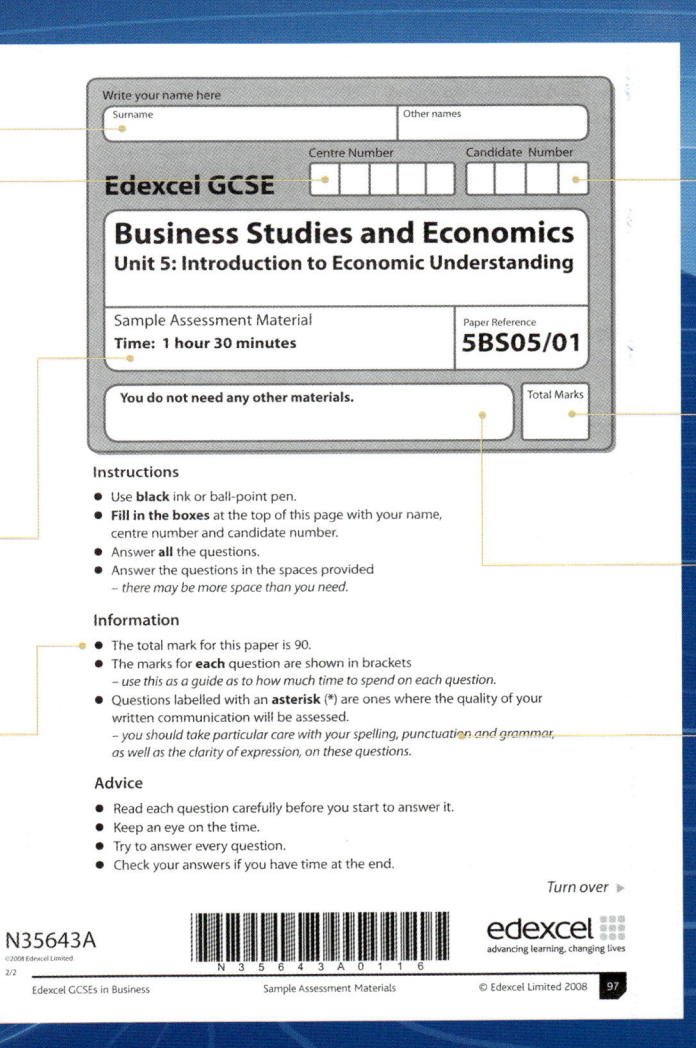

Here you fill in your personal exam number. Take care when writing it down because the number is important to the exam board when writing your score.

In this box, the examiner will write the total marks you have achieved in the exam paper.

Make sure you understand what you are allowed to take into the exam and what you are not.

Make sure that you understand exactly which questions you should attempt and the style you should use to answer them.

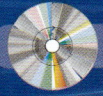

Edexcel GCSE

Business Studies and Economics
Unit 5: Introduction to Economic Understanding

Sample Assessment Material
Time: 1 hour 30 minutes

Paper Reference
5BS05/01

You do not need any other materials.

Instructions
- Use **black** ink or ball-point pen.
- **Fill in the boxes** at the top of this page with your name, centre number and candidate number.
- Answer **all** the questions.
- Answer the questions in the spaces provided
  – there may be more space than you need.

Information
- The total mark for this paper is 90.
- The marks for **each** question are shown in brackets
  – use this as a guide as to how much time to spend on each question.
- Questions labelled with an **asterisk** (*) are ones where the quality of your written communication will be assessed.
  – you should take particular care with your spelling, punctuation and grammar, as well as the clarity of expression, on these questions.

Advice
- Read each question carefully before you start to answer it.
- Keep an eye on the time.
- Try to answer every question.
- Check your answers if you have time at the end.

N35643A

More on the Active Teach CD

Zone Out

This section provides answers to the most common questions students have about what happens after they complete their exams. For much more information, visit www.examzone.co.uk

About your grades

Whether you've done better than, worse than or just as you expected, your grades are the final measure of your performance on your course and in the exams. On this page we explain some of the information that appears on your results slip and tell you what to do if you think something is wrong. We answer the most popular questions about grades and look at some of the options facing you.

When will my results be published?

Results for summer examinations are issued on the middle two Thursdays in August, with GCE first and GCSE second. January exam results are issued in March.

Can I get my results online?

Visit www.resultsplusdirect.co.uk, where you will find detailed student results information including the 'Edexcel Gradeometer' which demonstrates how close you were to the nearest grade boundary. Students can only gain their results online if their centre gives them permission to do so.

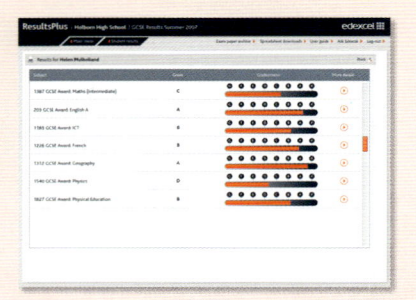

I haven't done as well as I expected. What can I do now?

First of all, talk to your subject teacher. After all the teaching that you have had, tests and internal examinations, he/she is the person who best knows what grade you are capable of achieving. Take your results slip to your subject teacher, and go through the information on it in detail. If you both think that there is something wrong with the result, the school or college can apply to see your completed examination paper and then, if necessary, ask for a re-mark immediately. The original mark can be confirmed or lowered, as well as raised, as a result of a re-mark.

How do my grades compare with those of everybody else who sat this exam?

You can compare your results with those of others in the UK who have completed the same examination using the information on our website at: http://www.edexcel.com

I achieved a higher mark for the same unit last time. Can I use that result?

Yes. The higher score is the one that goes towards your overall grade. The best result will be used automatically when the overall grade is calculated. You do not need to ask us to take into account a previous result. This will be done automatically so you can be assured that all your best unit results have gone into calculating your overall grade.

What happens if I was ill over the period of my examinations?

If you become ill before or during the examination period you are eligible for special consideration. This also applies if you have been affected by an accident, bereavement or serious disturbance during an examination.

If my school has requested special consideration for me, is this shown on my Statement of Results?

If your school has requested special consideration for you, it is not shown on your results slip, but it will be shown on a subject mark report that is sent to your school or college. If you want to know whether special consideration was requested for you, you should ask your Examinations Officer.

Can I have a re-mark of my examination paper?

Yes, this is possible, but remember that only your school or college can apply for a re-mark, not you or your parents/carers. First of all, you should consider carefully whether or not to ask your school or college to make a request for a re-mark. You should remember that very few re-marks result in a change to a grade - not because Edexcel is embarrassed that a change of marks has been made, but simply because a re-mark request has shown that the original marking was accurate.

Check the closing date for remarking requests with your Examinations Officer.

When I asked for a re-mark of my paper, my subject grade went down. What can I do?

There is no guarantee that your grades will go up if your papers are remarked. They can also go down or stay the same. After a re-mark, the only way to improve your grade is to take the examination again. Your school or college Examinations Officer can tell you when you can do that.

How many times can I resit a unit?

You may resit any unit in the Business Studies range once only. Most schools will cover the core unit 1 and 2 in year 10. This means that you could re-sit these assessments again – Unit 1 has re-sits in January and June and Unit 2 in June only. If you wish to re-sit one of the optional units, Units 3, 4 or 5, you can but it may be that you will have to wait until June in year 12 to do so. Some centres may teach the optional units in year 10 first but as a general rule this is unlikely.

For much more information, visit www.examzone.co.uk

More on the Active Teach CD

Index

Page references which appear in colour are defined in the Key Terms sections in each chapter.

A

Absolute poverty 100
Average cost 34, 58, 59
Alcohol
 reducing consumption of 48

B

Backward vertical integration 56
Ban 93
Benefits of decisions 20
Bulk-buying economies of scale 59
Business decisions 9
Business ethics 30
Business failure 32-35
Business growth 54-57

C

Cash flow 33
Charities 109
Choice 8
 and monopoly 63
Cigarettes
 reducing consumption of 48
Claimant count of unemployment 39
Competitive advantage 29
Competitiveness 29
Competition Commission 16, 66
Conflicts of interest 17
Congestion 85
Conglomerate merger 56
Consumer confidence 36
Consumer Price Index 37, 37-38
Corporate social responsibility 89
Corporate Social Responsibility report 29, 31
Cost of living 37
Costs of decisions 20
Customers
 as stakeholders 16

D

Debt 108
Debt relief 109
Demand 12, 33, 36
Differentiation 93-94
Diseconomies of scale 60
Diversified industry 109
Dividends 16

E

Economic activity 36, 46
Economic growth 77
    and sustainability 88-91
    drawbacks of 84
    problems of 84-87
Economies of scale 54, 58
Economist 8
Environmental awareness 30-31
Environmentally friendly 89
Equality 100
Ethical responsibility 89
Ethically responsible 110
EU regulation 68
Exchange rate 42
Exchange rates 42-45
Expectations 38
Exports 42
External growth 54, 55, 56
External shock 38
Externalities 20, 20-22
    and economic growth 85

F

Fairtrade 110
Fiscal policy 46
Financial Services Authority 68
Foreign consumers 37
Forward vertical integration 56
Free trade 105, 109
Friend of the Earth 89

G

GDP per capita 80
Globalisation 60
Government choices 9-10
Government
    and economic growth 78, 92-95
    and less economically developed
        countries 108
    and monopoly 62
    and poverty 100
    and solving economic problems 46-51
    as stakeholder 16
Government receipts 47
Government spending 47
Grants 78
Greenwash 89
Gross Domestic Product (GDP) 76
Growth
    of businesses 54-57, 58-61
    of the economy 76-79

H

Habits 48
Horizontal integration 56
Human capital investment 77

I

Imports 42
Incentives 93
Income inequalities 81, 101

Index

Independent Press Complaints Commission 68
Infant mortality rates 81
Inflation 37
Infrastructure 78
Innovation 55
Interest rate 46
Interest rates 36, 47
Internal growth 54
Internalising an externality 93
Internal shock 38, 38-39
International debt 108
International trade 104, 104-107

J

Jobseeker's allowance 3

L

Labour Force Survey measure of unemployment 39
Legislation 93
    and growth 92
Less economically developed countries (LECDs) 78, 81
Life expectancy rates 82
Literacy rates 82
Local community
    as stakeholder 16
Local monopoly 63

M

Market power 59, 62
Market share 28, 28-29, 54
Marketing mix 33
    and growth 54
Means-tested benefits 100
Merger 55
Monetary policy 46
Monopoly 62, 62-65,
Multinational corporations 106, 106-107

N

Natural monopoly 64
Necessity 13
Negative externalities 20, 21-22
    and economic growth 85
New product development 55
    and monopoly 63
NHS 48
Non-Government Organisations 109
Non-renewable resources 85
Non-tariff barriers 105

O

Office of Communications (OFCOM) 67
Office of Fair trading (OFT) 66
Office of Rail Regulation (ORR) 67
Office of the Water Regulator (OWAT) 67
Opportunity cost 9
Organic growth 54
Output 77

P

Physical capital investment 77
Place 33
Pollution 86,
Population growth 109
Portman Group 68
Positive externalities 21, 22
    and economic growth 85
Poverty 100
Poverty cycle 102
Poverty line 100
Pressure group 69
Pressure groups 68-69
Price 12, 12-15
    and monopoly 63
Price insensitivity 13, 93
Price sensitivity 13, 14
Privatisation 66
Productivity 34, 77
Profits 28
    and monopoly 63-64
Promotion 33
Protectionism 105
Public interest 68

Q

Quotas 105
Quality of life 81

R

Regulation 93
    and EU 68
    and large businesses 66-68
    and growth 92
Regulators 66
Relative poverty 102
Renewable resources 88
Research and development 55
Resources 77
Revenue 12
Risk 58

S

Scarcity 8
Self-regulation 68
Shareholders 16
Single European market 106
Size of the economy 76
Social performance 29
Social problems 47-48
Social success 29
Stakeholder model 17
Standard of living 80, 80-83
Stakeholders 16, 16-19
    and exchange rates 44
Strengthening pound 43-44
Strong pound 43-44
Substitute 13
Subsidies 92
Subsidy 93
Success 28-31

Index

Survival 58
Sustainable economic growth 88

T

Tariffs 105
Tax revenue 39
Taxation 47-48, 92
Taxes 92
Takeover 56

Technical economies of scale 59
Third party 20
    and growth 85
Trade-off 8, 8-11, 94
Transnational corporations 106, 106-107

U

Unemployment 39
Universal benefits 100

V

Value for money
    and monopoly 63
Vehicle excise duty 92
Vertical integration 56

W

Wage-price spiral 38
Warm Front Scheme 94
Waste 85
Weakening pound 43-44
Weak pound 43-44
Welfare state 100
Workers
    as stakeholders 16
World Bank 108
World Trade Organisation 110